Two Stars for Peace

Two Stars for Peace

✦

The Case for Using U.S. Statehood to Achieve Lasting Peace in the Middle East

Martine Rothblatt

iUniverse, Inc.
New York Lincoln Shanghai

Two Stars for Peace
The Case for Using U.S. Statehood to Achieve Lasting Peace in the Middle East

iUniverse, Inc.

For information address:
iUniverse
2021 Pine Lake Road, Suite 100
Lincoln, NE 68512
www.iuniverse.com

ISBN: 0-595-29288-7 (pbk)
ISBN: 0-595-65982-9 (cloth)

Printed in the United States of America

Dedication

This book is dedicated to young people of action, vision, and ethics.

All hundreds of millions of you!

Contents

Maps Credit

The Rhodes Armistice Line, 1949

Partitioned Jerusalem, 1948-1967

Courtesy of H.M. Sachar and PASSIA (www.passia.org)

Acknowledgements

My principal acknowledgement goes to Prof. Raymond Dwek of Oxford University. His creative pursuit of Middle East peace, which he does on top of a full-time job as head of the world's largest biochemistry department, was a great source of inspiration to me. His courage to solve water-rights issues with desalinization technology encouraged me also to think "outside the box." His willingness to address tough issues in the London media gave me the confidence to do so in this book.

Among the many other persons to whom thanks are due, I'd like to mention in particular Prof. Len Doyal, Ashraf al-Saeed, Paul Mahon, Rachel Turow, Robert Daye, Paul Rosenthal, Patrice French, Fred Hadeed, and Bina Aspen. Each of them has helped to develop my thinking or writing.

The astute reader will notice that I use alphabetical order when mentioning multiple ethnicities, nationalities, or religions in a single sentence. Also, despite editorial advice to the contrary, I occasionally use non-gendered third-person plural pronouns for gendered third-person singular pronouns. I prefer the flow and gender-neutrality of this grammatical usage. Finally, there are occasional, intended, changes of voice in the book. This is because the book is as much an objective, detached assessment of the Middle East situation as it is my own manifesto and passionate call to action.

Preface

I have none of the usual qualifications to write a book of geopolitical import—I'm not a diplomat, a politician, or a professor. I am, however, experienced with international relations. In 1987, as head of a satellite-communications company, I led an international effort that resulted in 183 countries signing a treaty permitting foreign satellites to provide mobile communications services in their territories. Five years later, in 1992, I led a similar effort that resulted in 175 countries signing a treaty that permitted satellites to transmit digital radio across national borders. Initially, almost everyone said these achievements would be impossible because they presented an affront to national sovereignty. However, I believed that the tangible benefits, such as cell phones and digital music, would outweigh those of keeping borders closed. I also doubted people would really believe these technologies could affect sovereignty issues.

Over some twenty years now I have launched challenging international projects that, despite many obstacles, were in fact realized. These projects have brought small-dish satellite communications to the entire world (PanAmSat) and global-positioning services to handheld devices (Geostar), buses (Humminbird GPS) and trucks. I have been honored to start the companies that today bring distance-learning channels to Asia and Africa (WorldSpace) and satellite radio to cars (Sirius; XM). My current project is the development of a medicine to open up the blood vessels of people who would otherwise face death, transplantation, or amputation due to non-operable blockages. Today this medicine, called Remodulin, is used across the globe, from Poland to Palestine and from Israel to Illinois. It is from this background of pragmatic conceptualization and successful implementation that I claim the right to propose a solution to the ongoing problem of Middle-East peace.

The solution involves no invention or discovery. It has always been there for everyone to see. But it lies in a place that nobody looks: the U.S. Constitution. Article 4, section 3 proclaims, "Congress may add additional states to the Union by majority vote." I propose that the peoples of Israel and Palestine petition the U.S. Congress to admit their lands as the 51st and 52nd states of the United States. I am confident that the U.S. Congress will agree, because doing so will remove a powder keg of instability that poses a huge threat to the American way of life. I believe that the peoples of Israel, Palestine, and the United States will reap tangible benefits of peace and prosperity—these are what national sovereignty is really all about.

This solution to the Middle East conundrum will seem obvious to some and ludicrous to others. The detractors will largely come from those quarters most threatened by union with America—instruments of stand-alone nationhood in Israel, agitators for stand-alone nationhood in Palestine, and arbiters of stand-alone nationhood in the diplomatic corps. Logically, they understand that unification with America makes them no less important and very much more safe and well-off. But logic persuades few addicts to give up their habits. Those who have spent a lifetime mainlining stand-alone nationhood will find withdrawal from it very hard to endure.

On the other hand, there are legions of youthful and open minds that ache at the madness of being sent into an unsolvable, life-long geopolitical maze. What young Israelis can look forward to seeing themselves, their children, and their grandchildren swimming in a sea of enmity no less bitter than the hatred surrounding their own grandfathers since before 1948? What young Palestinian can look forward to a life where their only choices are statelessness, Bantustan statehood, oppression, or suicide? This millennial generation will see unification with America as an idea whose time has come. This solution is the only way Israelis and Palestinians can win in the game of life. Living with pride and security as citizens of new American states of Palestine and Israel is the path of progress. It trumps every other game plan.

It is primarily to the youth of Israel, Palestine, and America that this book is addressed. Your minds are free. Your lives are before you. Take to the streets, peacefully, and demand Two Stars for Peace. Talk to your leaders, persuasively, and claim Two Stars for Peace. Stop all else that you are doing and insist upon Two Stars for Peace.

Introduction

The word "impossible" already seems to have disappeared from the language of technology. If a man who lived in the last century returned to Earth, he would find our whole life full of incomprehensible magic...To build a city it now takes us as many years as it required centuries at an earlier stage of history; America offers countless examples of this. The obstacle of distance has been overcome. The storehouse of the modern spirit already contains immeasurable riches. Every day this wealth increases; a hundred thousand minds think and search at every point of the globe, and what one discovers belongs to the whole of the world the next moment.

—Theodore Herzl, *The Jewish State*, 1896.

The drama and trauma of today's Middle East has its genesis in Theodore Herzl's 1896 pamphlet, *The Jewish State*. Much of Herzl's reasoning is forgotten today. Here is a thumbnail sketch:

- The root cause of discrimination is the human tendency to place fault, which is manifested in societies as scapegoating—the attribution of undeserved fault to a visible minority group.

- If Jews are not in a majority somewhere, they will be doomed to everlasting discrimination everywhere.

- Assimilation will never end discrimination because resistance of most non-Jews to intermarriage and the refusal of many Jews to assimilate makes total assimilation impossible.

- Assimilation should never be the goal, because it entails the self-immolation of a beautiful culture.

- It doesn't matter whether the Jewish-majority state is in Palestine, Argentina, or any place between.

1

- A Jewish-majority state should be a secular state founded upon labor rights, and its flag should have seven gold stars on a white background to represent a seven-hour work day and a pure spirit.

- Jews are, in general, no different from other peoples, especially in terms of basic human nature.

Based on these and a hundred other arguments, momentum grew during the early twentieth-century for a Jewish state. The emotional power of the Holocaust provided the necessary push to finally birth the country of Israel. Most of Herzl's predictions and visions failed to materialize. However, his core belief that a Jewish-majority homeland was possible was vindicated. Of course, such a place would be free of anti-Jewish discrimination, since Jews would be in power and not subject to scapegoating.

Here are some considerations Herzl failed to identify:

- Visible minorities among the Jews, such as those from non-European backgrounds, would remain subject to discrimination for the same reasons anti-Semitism thrived in Europe.

- A Jewish state anywhere would have to exist in a sea of non-Jewish neighboring states and hence, in this larger context, Jews would remain subjects of hatred and scapegoating.

- Indigenous and immigrating non-Jewish peoples in the Jewish state would themselves become victims of discrimination and scapegoating, leading to a discontented "fifth column" within the Jewish state.

- The United States would emerge as a "nation of minorities," in which, after decades of civil-rights growing pains, anti-Semitism would virtually disappear despite the fact that the U.S. hosted by far the largest Jewish population in the world.

I believe that Herzl would have been impressed with the "nation of minorities" that is the United States today. I believe he would have envisioned the Jewish state as being a member of the American federation, much as Utah was originally envisioned as a Mormon safe-haven state. My belief is made even stronger when I consider the pain Herzl would have felt at the knowledge that Israel must constantly battle enemies, both domestic and external. He would have seen such warfare as good for building Israeli identity, but detrimental to building a quality life for Jews.

The Israeli situation of today is not the best solution to the age-old problem of anti-Semitism. Things are, of course, much better than in the days when no place had a Jewish majority. However, the status quo constantly destroys the quality of Jewish life, both directly and reflexively (the trauma inflicted upon their Palestinian neighbors). Herzl envisioned Israel as a model for the world, but today most of the world associates Israel with tanks and military bulldozers. There is a better way.

By trading sovereignty for American statehood, Israel will come out far ahead. There will be no greater risk of anti-Semitism. For many Jewish sub-groups, there may well be less discrimination thanks to the ever-expanding civil-rights protections of the U.S. Constitution. With American statehood there will be less insecurity, for Israel will now be defended without apology or concession-haggling by the only superpower. As part and parcel of America, Israel will fully realize Herzl's dream of a Jewish majority state that serves as a shining cultural, scientific, and industrial example to the world.

As successful a geopolitical solution as an Israeli State of America would be, it is a chimera without the simultaneous admission of a Palestinian State of America. Every benefit the Israelis seek—peace, security, quality of life—is sought as well by their Palestinian siblings. Every tenet of logic that supports a Jewish state—majority population, recognizable boundaries, historical claims—supports a Palestinian state as well.

The Palestinian people have lived under a long succession of alien rulers. Their aspiration for sovereignty in a homeland is a noble, justifiable cause. Most of the people who arrive as immigrants on America's shores have suffered similar oppression, sometimes political, other times ethnic or economic. Whether one's oppression is from a distant Ottoman, a rigid church, or a lofty caste, the aspiration for liberty is no less acute. America has provided countless ethnic, religious, and socioeconomic groups with sovereign lives via freedom to associate, freedom to worship, freedom to learn, and freedom to earn. Many Palestinians have rescued their lives from oppression by starting new lives on America's shores.

However, Palestinian aspirations go even beyond those of other groups who have found satisfaction by establishing new communities in the U.S. Most Palestinians still live in or near the ancestral homeland. They neither desire to move nor is it possible to remove them. To do so would run afoul of Herzl's admonition against the abandonment of beautiful cultures, for while the cultural plant may be transplanted, it grows with special beauty in its native soil. There is, however, an ideal way to bring truly sovereign lives to the Palestinian people—that is by bringing America to Palestine via the establishment of a Palestinian State of America.

By joining the United States, the Palestinian people will be able to enjoy the same sovereign lives as their brothers and sisters already living in America. In addition, however, they will reap the ultimate reward of enjoying that sovereignty in the beautiful land of their ancestors. The bureaucratic particularities of sovereignty are of little concern to the common person. What the Palestinian wants to know is: "Am I respected as an equal citizen of my country? Am I entitled to travel, work, and learn where I want to within my country? Will I be safe and secure within my country? Does my country include the birthplace of my father and his grandfather?" To all of these questions, the answer is a resounding "yes."

An outline of the situation has been presented. Currently, people speak of "two-state" solutions. I propose instead a "two-star" solution: Two Stars for Peace. When America welcomes Israel and Palestine as the 51st and 52nd states of the Union, the age-old dream of peace and prosperity in the land of milk and honey will have been achieved. As America re-sews her flag with a 51st and 52nd star, the entire world will applaud the arrival of this fine new design. For the Middle East will appear on the world stage as a place of stability and understanding, and tensions everywhere will be visibly reduced. Men and women everywhere will look at Israelis and Palestinians with admiration, and Americans will take well-deserved pride in the awesome potential of their new citizens.

1

The Problem

The peace process itself in a way self-negated because no single agreement was honored completely. No single timetable was adhered to. No single commitment was implemented—either on time or fully. There was constant, constant haggling, delays, postponements. And in the meantime, Israel would annex more land, confiscate more land, build more settlements…We need our own land returned to us, the territory occupied in 1967. But the causes of the conflict have to be addressed. Jerusalem has to be returned. The refugees have the right to return. They cannot be totally deprived of the protection of the law, which protects other people. How come when it comes to the Palestinians, we have to relinquish those rights, and we have to be made to sign an agreement, which will only lead to further conflict?…American long-term interests have to be translated into a strategic, responsible, even-handed view of what is needed in peace…And either there's a responsibility and the courage, the integrity and the willingness to abide by international law, to create a just peace, or we cannot be punished by a punitive peace process, which is unjust and that will prepare the grounds for perpetual conflict.

—Hanan Ashrawi, *McNeil News Hour,* October 31, 2000

We are foreordained or doomed, however you want to put it, to live together. Otherwise you have permanent apartheid, à la South Africa, and permanent conflict.

—Hanan Ashrawi, *Christian Science Monitor,* June 7, 2002

Imagine a map of the world in which each country was the size of its relative share of news coverage. The Middle East would occupy almost half the globe. Why is the media obsessed with the Middle East? First, a lot of violence occurs there (violence always draws a crowd). Second, people of Islamic, Christian, and Jewish faiths care about what goes on in one of their religious homelands. Third, the Middle East lies at the junction of Europe, Asia, and Africa. What happens there can affect vast regions of the world.

The Middle East remains in the news because it has the characteristics of a "perfect conflict"—one that never ends. History vested two different peoples with overlapping rights to the same piece of geography. How could conflict not result? Each side has vast resources to tap outside the contested lands. How can the conflict ever burn itself out? Religious imagery employed by the combatants acts like a force field, keeping foreign armies away. How can the conflict ever get snuffed out? The problem of Middle-East peace is one of breaking out of the conditions that cause never-ending warfare.

Overlapping Histories

The hand of time writes history in the margins of its previous volumes. Events periodically permit this overlapping text to be transcribed into a new volume, with clear margins. The transcription still reflects the scribbles and cross-outs of history, but it does so with an editor's flair for coherence. This new state of affairs will itself soon be littered with margin notes, leading the entire process to repeat itself.

The peoples of the Middle East, and interested persons everywhere, read from different books of time. Even those who read from the same book come to different conclusions about the meanings of ambiguities introduced by clever editors to bridge recent marginalia with ancient text. There is no current account that enjoys general agreement, for the world is kaleidoscopic. Instead, different groups of people look at the same geography, refer to their own book of reality, and recite out loud, "We must fight for what is ours." When different books claim that a single piece of land is entitled to different "ours," and when the editors of these books say "might makes right," conflict is inevitable. And so it has been, for thousands of years.

The problem of conflicting histories arises because the hand of time writes without thinking of the future. Peoples are swept off a land and pulled back onto it. Peoples are handed the best of a land and then pushed to its margins. Peoples are granted dominion and then shown discrimination. But while time writes eclectically, its etchings are never lost. The course of events is inscribed in the memes of a people. The moral compass that resides in the souls of people causes them to cry out for rationality. Writers and politicians, leaders and commoners, all cry out for fairness. And so the masses struggle to control the hand of time. People grab it by the wrist, the forearm, the shoulder, and demand that it write consistently with the books of history.

"Which book of history?" laughs Time, as it scribbles more wildly than ever before, tugged and jerked by proponents of a hundred different editions of reality.

Which book indeed? It is not possible to write consistently with a multiplicity of conflicting storylines, many developed over the course of centuries, in relay-race fashion, by hundreds of well-intended but far-from-prescient editors. Only God knows where Time ultimately leads, and prophets of the same God must have shared with us the same message. It is we, the hapless humans, who have gotten things horribly confused.

Conflicting Claims of Sovereignty

There will be no peace so long as conflicting books of time determine earthly sovereignty over Jerusalem and its surrounding lands. It is not possible for two or more people to safely steer a car. This is the core problem of the Middle East—one area of Earth, those lands which surround Jerusalem, is subject to two conflicting claims of sovereignty.

The Israeli claim of sovereignty has behind it the force of international law, which created its borders in 1948, and the force of military might in the West Bank and Gaza. It also enjoys the weight of biblical history, a century of cultivated development, and the world's empathy for its efforts to achieve security. The Palestinian claim of sovereignty has the probity of a historical presence that reaches centuries back in time, far beyond the mandates of the United Nations. It is bolstered by the commanding presence of several million current occupants, modern international law's recognition of their right to self-determination, and the world's empathy for their efforts to achieve freedom from state-of-siege conditions.

The root problem of the Middle East is that two different groups have been given sovereignty over more-or-less the same expanse of land. One can argue the details as to whose sovereign rights are more legitimate or more recent or more compelling. Such arguments will never persuade those who believe in the other's claim of sovereignty. Humans are great at believing what they want to believe.

From these competing claims of sovereignty flows the fuel that keeps hatred burning in the Middle East. Sovereignty includes the right to pass and enforce laws. Under Israeli sovereignty, laws are passed that infuriate Palestinians. Similarly, in places where Palestinians have control, they do or say things that inflame Israeli passions. There is no single sovereignty that has the respect and participation of both peoples. Consequently, the battle rages on and on.

Here is a metaphor for the Middle East: Imagine a dirt lot in a working-class urban neighborhood. The man who originally owned the lot willed it exclusively for use by boys who want to play football. Generations of local boys played football on the lot, and neighborhood teams became a deep-seated tradition. Many years later a city agency claimed the lot in the public interest and decreed that it be used solely for co-educational baseball. Boys and girls arrived in city buses daily to compete in municipal baseball leagues. The same piece of land was subject to different sets of rules—football versus baseball. Before long, all the kids were fighting each other in football-versus-baseball wars instead of playing sports. It is simply not possible to play baseball and football at the same time on a single dirt lot. Similarly, it is simply not possible to have two different sovereignties, each with its own unique and generally conflicting set of laws, on the same tract of Holy Land.

Illusions

It is equally unrealistic for one interpretation of reality to self-immolate in favor of another. Memes, like genes, can be extraordinarily persistent. Evolution does not favor shrinking violets, nor does history favor self-effacing cultures. If either Israelis or Palestinians were of the shy sort, there would be no Middle-East conflict today. Instead, we are talking about great peoples grappling with the harsh and conflicting realities that have emerged from the inscrutable text of time.

Geographical gerrymandering will also fail to solve the core problem. The approach of declaring two side-by-side sovereignties gives only the illusion of enabling two competing realities to co-exist at peace. In fact, Jerusalem and its greater environs form a single ecosystem, as well as a hybrid socio-cultural matrix, neither of which can be fairly parsed. In such situations, the weaker entity takes what it can get, realizing that doing so gives it a platform from which to reach further next time around. The stronger entity pats itself on the back, thinking its problem is solved. Instead, almost immediately the absurdly sewn suit begins to unravel at the seams.

Youth in the economically depressed stump-state will blame their problems on the unfair distribution of geography at the time of parsing. They will use agitation to extend their borders, since that will appear more likely to produce results than working within the meager resources of take-it-or-leave-it boundaries. Both parties will have lost yet another generation to conflict.

With Israeli authority now setting the rules, the Palestinians must fight for self-determination. With the two populations roughly equal in numbers and steadfast in pride, neither will ever acquiesce to the other's control. The current popular solution, two side-by-side sovereignties, is a chimera. The unitary nature of the land admits but one sovereign. Any circumvention of this reality will be short-term. A Bantustan-like Palestine will be economically defective and politically humiliated by its overbearing Israeli neighbor. After a couple of years, a new *intifada* will arise, this time with the longer and stronger arms afforded by a stump-state sovereign.

An escape from the mad maze of Middle-East politics does exist. But we must be like the character in Edwin Abbot's *Flatland*, who looked to the third dimension for his escape. By thinking "outside the box" of two sovereign peoples and one piece of holy land, we can find a lasting solution that brings peace and pride. It is to this unseen escape hatch that we now turn.

American Involvement

America can cut the Gordian knot of Middle-East peace, but not with military assistance, economic bribery, or photo-op summit meetings. None of these tools have worked in the past. There is no reason to expect that they will work in the future. None of these tools address the root problem: two competing claims of sovereignty over a single piece of land.

Military assistance is about smashing dissenters into submission. But none of the mighty empires of history could smash either the Jewish or the Palestinian peoples into submission. Surely these peoples may bow for a time, just as a tree inherently knows it is better to bow before a strong wind. However, there is no gale force on earth that can wipe all trees from existence. Trees, like oppressed peoples, scatter their seeds far and wide and promptly re-root and flourish as soon as conditions permit. U.S. military assistance can make the difference in eliminating a shallow threat. However, there is nothing shallow about Palestinian aspirations. The roots of these people run as deep as their tenure on the land is long. The strength of their roots is measured by the depth and breadth of their cultural traditions, many of which sprawl over every aspect of life.

Multi-billion dollar carrots are also ineffectual in producing lasting change. Such big numbers impress leaders and businessmen. Not surprisingly, grants-in-aid are the principal lubricant for getting plenipotentiaries to sign noble agreements. The dollars are, at best, abstractions to the masses. At worst, they are an admission of a bad deal. Does a butcher pay you to take away a lamb shank? Of course not. Only the garbage of a shop requires a payment for its removal.

There is a funny notion among diplomats that political problems can be made to disappear by persuading leaders to compromise. This view made sense in Bismarck's time, when monarchs ruled absolutely. In today's age it is antiquated, because the masses are no longer inextricably tied to their king. Today, when a leader makes a deal with another leader, each is hoping they can "sell" the deal to their peoples. Sometimes they can, especially if the issue is not perceived as important, such as greenhouse-emission limitations twenty years into the future. But when the deals involve the sovereignty of a people, the days are long gone when a leader's compromises mean much to their people, especially if the deal compromises their future. The disgruntled will simply continue to agitate for what they believe is right.

It is therefore not surprising that "summit diplomacy," "shuttle diplomacy," and "spirit-of-you-name-it diplomacy" have all failed to achieve peace in the Middle East. These diplomatic efforts invariably bypass the core problem of two conflicting sovereignties in the same geography. Instead, they seek to get the leaders of each people to "compromise" on the extent or scope of their sovereignty. Even when the leaders agree, their peoples do not. The people feel the pain of thousands of "devil-in-the-details" implications that arise when an attempt is made to shoehorn two competing sovereignties into one geography. Leaders and diplomats gloss over these rough points, either because they are uninterested in details, they are too pressed for time, or they are anxious for an apparent success.

The fact is that we are now in an age of human rights. International law is changing to recognize the standing of individuals, and certainly of large groups of individuals. The destinies of great peoples can no longer be bartered and negotiated in the manner of the former European powers, who swapped swaths of Africa amongst themselves. Consequently, while "photo-op" summits are great media events, they utterly fail to address the core problems of the Middle East. In order for a solution to work it must make sense to the vast majority of the Palestinian and Israeli people. No such solution is possible if it is constrained by the maintenance of two sovereign governments in one small piece of land.

America does have a solution to offer directly to the Israeli and Palestinian people. It will take courage on the part of America and careful study on the part of the Israelis and Palestinians. After such study, however, the benefits will be so apparent that the people will demand this solution. Here is how America can stop contributing to the problem and start solving it:

- Announce that Israel and Palestine are invited to join the great federation as its 51st and 52nd states;

- Set reasonable conditions and provide meaningful guarantees for their admission that resolve the major fears and concerns of each people; and

- Instruct the State Department to work closely with the Arab World, European Union, and other interested parties, especially the UN, so that inaccurate perceptions are quickly corrected.

Some may say that this is too much, way too much, American involvement in the Middle East. There is no option for less U.S. involvement. By virtue of its heartfelt importance to America's Christians, Jews, and Muslims, and its geopolitical strategic value, the Middle East must remain an area of American involvement. Its festering irresolution feeds terrorism the way an open wound feeds pathogenic bacteria.

In summary, the problem of America's involvement in the Middle East is not whether to be involved, but *how* to be involved. America is unavoidably involved. To date, her involvement has been well-intentioned but wholly dysfunctional. American weapons sold to Israel are used more often within Palestinian borders than against foreign armies. American financial aid glistens so brilliantly that it blinds Middle-Eastern leaders to the real underlying problems. American diplomacy makes for great entertainment. Like the mass media opiate that it is, once its magic wears off the hunger for a realpolitik fix rages more violently than ever.

After fifty years of false starts, it is time for a new form of American involvement, an involvement that successfully addresses the underlying problem of two sovereignties in one geography.

Effects of Failure

Imagine if the Middle-East situation continued on its current path for another fifty years. Today, there is a once-unthinkable wall going up around Israel. In another decade or two, the wall will show its porosity, and automation will diminish the need for Palestinian workers. What will be the reaction when terrorist acts become even more common and brazen? The once-unthinkable will become acceptable: forcible relocations of all Palestinians to east of the Jordan River. A purely Jewish state will be viewed as the only safe option.

Neighboring Arab countries will have to fight militarily to prevent such an outrage, but they will lose. They will also attempt to pressure America and Europe economically. But that too will likely be of diminishing value in the rapidly evolving cyber-technological economy. The combined humiliations of national expulsion, military defeat, and economic impotence will fuel apocalyptic efforts. Desperate men and women will try to wipe Israel out, once and for all, with black-market nuclear or biological weapons. They may well succeed, even though everyone else will lose. In a decade or two, mass death will have matured and will be possible to inflict with portable technology.

The apocalyptic war will also extend to Europe and America, because Israel is inextricably bound to intergovernmental Western pressure. Paris, London, Washington—no place will be safe from massive-scale death in decades to come, if New York City could be crippled in 2001. When we fail to drain the quicksand of Middle East politics, we all but ensure that those deepest in the muck, the Palestinians, will drag many others down into the hell below.

Clearly, failure is not an option. One definition of insanity is to keep doing the same thing while expecting a different result. Think of the insane man who pounds his head against the wall waiting for something magical to appear. Military assistance, financial assistance, diplomacy: these have all failed constantly over dozens of years, working only on paper, and never in reality, no matter how many permutations were tried.

It is high time to admit to failure of the past methods; but giving up is permanent failure, and it is not an option. The consequences would be cataclysmic, and it is unnecessary. There is a new way, a systematic solution, a resolution of the underlying problem of two sovereignties in one geography.

2

The Solution

Discovery consists of seeing what everybody has seen and thinking what nobody has thought.

—Albert von Szent-Gyorgi, 1962

We must indeed all hang together, or, most assuredly, we shall all hang separately.

—Benjamin Franklin, 1776

If men were angels, no government would be necessary. If angels were to govern men, neither external nor internal controls on government would be necessary. In framing a government which is to be administered by men over men, the great difficulty lies in this: you must first enable the government to control the governed, and in the next place oblige it to control itself. A dependence on the people is, no doubt, the primary control on the government, but experience has taught mankind the necessity of auxiliary precautions.

—James Madison, Federalist Papers, 1787

The American flag contains fifty stars. It has changed twenty-six times since 1777, when it was officially adopted and had thirteen. The principle has always been the same—add one star to the flag each time a state is added to the union. No star is larger or differently colored or preferentially positioned than any other star. This reflects the American commitment to equality between her states.

This book is entitled *Two Stars for Peace* because that is exactly what is needed. Israel and Palestine should be invited to join the United States as equal states in the union. Accordingly, every U.S. flag will be revised to contain fifty-two stars. This huge logistical effort is a small price to pay for the honor of welcoming the Holy Land into the United States of America. Every newly-stitched American flag will declare that peace has been achieved by embracing Israelis and Palestinians as American citizens and by welcoming their lands as separate, but equal, American states.

It has been forty-four years since the U.S. flag was modified to signify the admission of Hawaii. This is a long enough period of time for the admission process to be reawakened. An even longer forty-seven years transpired between the admission of New Mexico, in 1912, and Alaska, in 1959. The time is ripe to admit Two Stars for Peace.

American Statehood

America is a one-of-a-kind country. No other land is comprised of numerous unique territories that voluntarily elected to forego their own sovereignty in favor of being a part of a larger nation. This political innovation has prevented much potentially violent conflict among the many different peoples that settled the American frontier. The one instance that two different sovereignties did try to stand on the same land—the anti-slave North and the pro-slave South—resulted in the American Civil War. More Americans died in that conflict than the combined U.S. death toll from all other wars involving Americans.

Can we not analogize the situation of Israel and Palestine to that of the South and the North in the American Civil War? Two sovereignties superimposed upon an integral geographic space? Are not the constant battles between Israelis and Palestinians essentially a *civil* war? While this civil war cannot be resolved within a United States of the Middle East—for no such entity exists—it can be resolved by adding Israeli and Palestinian states to a slightly enlarged United States of America.

The Founding Fathers of the American Republic foresaw the benefits of growing the country by voluntary association. Enshrined in article 4, section 3 of the U.S. Constitution is the following statement: "Congress may add additional states to the Union by majority vote." The U.S. Congress has usually taken these majority votes only upon receipt of a petition from the elected leaders of another country or territory. In over 200 years of taking such votes, the U.S. Congress has only once definitively rejected a petition for statehood.[1]

---

1. In 1993, the House of Representatives rejected the petition of the seat of federal government, the District of Columbia, to become its own state. However, the 23rd Amendment to the U.S. Constitution, adopted in 1961, did give the District three presidential electors. This actually provides District residents with a proportionally greater vote in presidential elections than residents of more populous states. Each District presidential elector represents about 200,000 voters, whereas each California presidential elector represents about 600,000 voters. See Chapter 3 for a further dis-cussion of the effect of the Two Stars Plan on presidential electors. Congress initially failed to approve statehood overtures from Texas, Wyoming, and a few other states due to transient political considerations, but within a few years mustered the neces-sary votes and granted them statehood.

Israel and Palestine can become American states simply by having their duly-elected representatives send a Petition for Statehood to the U.S. Congress. Of course, such an action would follow from referenda or party caucuses among the Israeli and Palestinian people, as well as extensive grassroots lobbying and educational efforts. The statehood petition would be addressed to the Speaker of the House of Representatives. It would say something along the following lines:

"We, the duly elected representatives of the people of [Israel/Palestine] do hereby request admission as a state in the United States of America."

"We understand the obligations of American statehood and citizenship and hereby attest to our willingness to meet those obligations."

"We forward herewith a draft State Constitution which is wholly consistent with the U.S. Constitution."

"We respectfully request favorable consideration from the U.S. Congress, on behalf of the American people."

With these words, the Israeli and Palestinian peoples would launch the ship of their salvation. Their states would assuredly be welcome. The U.S. Congress would grant a warm welcome, in the form of a Joint Resolution specifying key conditions and guarantees, because doing so would solve America's most intractable, and most material, foreign-affairs problem.

With a few strokes of a pen, state boundaries will be finalized, across which people will be able to move freely. The U.S. Senate and House of Representatives will be adjusted to include members elected from the new states of Israel and Palestine. Current elected representatives in Israel and Palestine will no doubt quickly populate the governors' mansions and state legislatures of those new American stars. Israeli and Palestinian defense forces will be reconstituted as federally-controlled National Guard units or integrated into the federal armed services. U.S. civil rights and non-discrimination laws will prevail. The long and strong arms of the U.S. federal government will guarantee order and security for all. There will be, at long last, peace in the lands surrounding Jerusalem: Two Stars for Peace.

Legal Boundaries

Today, much of the argument in the Middle East is over boundaries. How will these be settled in the context of U.S. statehood? With divine guidance, the Israelis and Palestinians have already answered this question. As will be shown below, their answer made no sense in the context of two superimposed sovereignties. However, it makes perfect sense when the two states are components of a single sovereign power, the United States.

Israel was once satisfied with the boundaries it received from the United Nations in 1948. The Arabs never were, and even the Israeli satisfaction faded fast when their indefensibility was demonstrated. Nevertheless, a pillar of Israeli foreign policy has always been that it will trade the land it conquered subsequent to its War of Independence for *true* peace and harmony. Specifically, Israel has repeatedly expressed its willingness to return to its pre-1967 boundaries (the Armistice boundaries of 1949) if it can be assured of complete security and normalcy. Indeed, its largest land conquest, the Sinai, was returned to Egypt when Anwar Sadat signed the Camp David peace treaty with Menachem Begin. The United Nations has enshrined its basis for peace in UN Security Council Resolution 242. This provides for Israel to withdraw to the pre-1967 borders (i.e., the 1949 Armistice borders) and for all states in the area to respect each other's territorial integrity.[2] The Palestinian leadership has now also accepted the 1949 Armistice borders.[3]

Israel has never felt the peace and harmony it desires. Consequently, it has never been willing to return to its pre-1967 borders. For example, Israel is unwilling to return the Golan Heights to Syria due to fears of bombardment from the area. It is equally unwilling to part with East Jerusalem for fear that the Israeli people will once again be precluded from worshipping at its holy sites.

---

2. UN Resolution 242 effectively grandfathers the changes in the Israeli-Palestinian borders that occurred after 1948. In other words, the pre-1967 borders, which are the same as the 1949 Armistice borders, replace those delineated in the UN General Assembly Resolution 181, which partitioned Israel and Palestine from the British mandate over the region. Nevertheless, the fuzziness of the situation exemplifies why the UN has an important role to play in the Two Stars Plan, as described in Chapter 9.

3. The 1949 Armistice borders provide the Palestinian Authority with approximately 5690 square kilometers on the West Bank and 365 square kilometers in the Gaza Strip, while leaving Israel with approximately 20,770 square kilometers. By way of comparison, under the UN Partition Plan in 1947, Israel received about 14,245 square kilometers and a planned Palestinian state received about 11,655 square kilo-meters. That Palestinian land now represents only about 22% of Israeli-Palestinian space explains why Palestinians call the UN Partition and subsequent Israeli War of Independence *al nakba*, or "the catastrophe." To make matters worse, soon after the Armistice, Jordan and Egypt promptly took over control of the remaining 22% (the West Bank and Gaza, respectively) not occupied by Israel, leaving Palestinians with nothing at all for a state, although Jordan did grant them Jordanian citizenship. After Israel conquered the remaining 22% in the 1967 Six Day War, Jordan and Egypt ceded these claims back to the Palestinians.

The Two Stars Plan assures Israel peace and harmony. As part of the United States, there will be no risk that Israel will be invaded by Syria, Jordan, or Egypt. As American citizens, there will be no risk that Israelis will be prevented from traveling to East Jerusalem—or to any other part of the United States, including anywhere in Palestine. Hence, Israel will agree to liberal borders for a neighboring Palestinian state because, as parts of the United States, each is precluded from continuing the hateful behavior toward the other that is currently being perpetrated. As part of the United States, a Palestinian state composed of Jordan's old holdings west of the Jordan River, plus Gaza, no longer presents a security threat to Israel. For this reason, Israel will agree to the 1949 Armistice line as its border with a neighboring, co-American Palestinian state.

On the other hand, there is no reason, in the context of the Two Stars Plan, for Israel to disgorge the Golan Heights. Palestinians do not populate this ex-Syrian territory. Whether or not the Golan Heights are ever returned to Syria will become, after U.S. statehood for Israel and Palestine, a matter for the U.S. government to decide. Given the strategic value of high ground, it seems improbable that this swath of territory will ever be wrestled away. Similarly, after annexation of Texas, the U.S. purchased some Texan-occupied Mexican border territory from Mexico, settling a long territorial dispute. The matter of the Golan Heights can be settled according to the precedent set by this earlier negotiation.

The status of Jewish settlements in Palestine is also resolved under the Two Stars Plan. They remain where they are. Even more may be built, as may Palestinian settlements in today's Israel. Of course, the laws of property must be respected, as has often not been the case to date. This legal compliance will be greatly enhanced under the U.S. judicial system.

In the United States, ethnicity or religion is irrelevant to where people may live or farm. While Utah is a predominantly Mormon state, it must respect the rights of people of different religions to live and farm there. Similarly, Mormons are welcome to live and farm outside Utah. The situation is no different for Jewish farmers in the West Bank. They will be residents of the state of Palestine and citizens of the United States. The Palestinian authorities must respect their rights no differently than the rights of any other resident.[4] Should the state of

---

4. Under legal precedent for similar situations in other annexed U.S. states, pre-statehood land ownership must be respected, even if obtained fraudulently. Thus, Jewish settlers with lawful title to their land in the West Bank must be permitted to stay, although they would become U.S. citizen residents of the American state of Palestine rather than of Israel. Lawsuits against Israel for improperly granting such title could be pursued through the U.S. federal courts. The U.S. government may wish to accept liability for any resulting claims, as it did with the claims of Texas residents against Mexico when Texas joined the U.S. See Chapter 10.

Palestine's police protection fall short, the U.S. federal government has the authority—and the obligation—to step in and protect the settler's rights.

Provided that settlers acquired their homestead in accordance with the law, any discriminatory action toward them would violate the U.S. Constitution's promise of "equal protection."

As one of the United States, Israel would not require more land than it owned prior to 1967. Palestine would not require more land than Israel conquered from Jordan in 1967, which has long been ceded by Jordan to a future Palestinian state. This means that the settlements that freckle the face of the West Bank today will be part and parcel of the new Palestinian State of America. On the other hand, there cannot be borders inhibiting the transit of Israelis to and from those settlements, nor of Palestinians moving between Israel and Palestine. Under U.S. law, passage between those two states can be no more complex than driving from Virginia to Maryland (although hopefully quicker than during rush hour!).

Would religious Jews like to establish a new settlement in Palestine? No longer will it be necessary to make an international incident out of the event. No longer will they have to wrangle a blind eye from the Israeli government and grow up under the nasty cloak of illegality. As with buyers and sellers of property in any other part of the United States, the settlers need simply reach mutually acceptable terms of accommodation with owners. Where and when such a real-estate deal closes, a settlement can occur. On the other hand, the bulldozing of Palestinian land rights with legal subterfuges could no longer be pulled off. As part of the U.S., an aggrieved Palestinian landowner has not only the Palestinian courts, but also U.S. Courts of Appeal from which to enjoin any problematic action against their property.

State Constitutions

There is a standard procedure by which a territory becomes an American state. It ordinarily involves three steps: (1) a petition from the territory or republic seeking U.S. statehood, (2) authorization by the U.S. President and Congress for the residents to draft a state constitution, and (3) approval of the new constitution by the House of Representatives, the U.S. Senate, and the President. This exact procedure need not be followed for Israel and Palestine, but it is important for the legislature of each to draft a new state constitution that is consistent with the U.S. Constitution.

There are both legal and practical reasons why Israelis and Palestinians need to develop state constitutions. In addition, the development and submission of such a draft constitution is the best means of signifying a state's intent to be part of the United States.

From a legal perspective, article 4, section 4 of the U.S. Constitution says that it is a federal obligation to ensure that all states have democratically-elected governments. In order for Congress to ensure this obligation is respected, there must be a democratically-oriented state constitution in place on day one.

Practically speaking, a good reason for the draft state constitutions is that the day after a state is admitted to the United States there must be a legal framework from which to govern that state. Without a draft constitution to look at, Congress would have no way to assure itself that the laws of the new state would be consistent with the laws of the United States.

Israelis and Palestinians do not, at this time, have formal national constitutions in place. Israel has proceeded along the British path of using a series of basic legal documents that, *in toto*, operate as a *de facto* constitution.[5] The Palestinian Constitution is in a draft form and is currently receiving expert legal feedback. In either case, there is no need to start from scratch. All that is needed is an adjustment of the existing documents to bring the language in line with that of an American state's constitution. Here are a few examples of the types of changes that would need to be made:

- Preambles should be changed to reflect the evolution to and reasons for American statehood;

- Terminology such as President, Prime Minister, Knesset, and National Assembly should be changed to more appropriate statehood monikers such as Governor and State Legislature and their Arabic and Hebrew equivalents;

- Powers that are inconsistent with American statehood, such as collecting duties, printing currency, and national defense, should be deleted;

- Powers that are needed under the U.S. Constitution, such as electing two U.S. Senators and apportioning Congressional districts, should be added;

---

5. Some scripturally religious Israelis object to the concept of a secular constitution for a Jewish state because they believe only sacred text can serve as one's constitution. In a similar vein, there is tension in draft Palestinian constitutions between providing a privileged position for Islam and contradicting that position with standard secular provisions. Both of these objections are resolved with the Two Stars Plan. Since nei-ther state may interfere with the free practice of religion, there is no conflict between having a wholly secular constitution and a citizen's separate, and even superior, obli-gations to their faith.

- Provisions that are inconsistent with the U.S. Constitution, such as state involvement in religion, should be avoided; and

- Rights of many kinds may be added, such as expanded privacy protections, for the U.S. Constitution reserves a great deal of power for states.

There is no doubt that it would be a big job to craft the Israeli and Palestinian proto-constitutional documents into U.S. state constitutions. However, it is not nearly as difficult as developing an original constitution for a stand-alone country. The U.S. Constitution, in addition to being the oldest surviving written constitution, provides clear guidance and boundaries.[6] Fortunately, there are highly-capable Israeli and Palestinian legal scholars who can prepare initial drafts. There are software programs that compare all fifty existing state constitutions, thus enabling Israel and Palestine to readily pick and choose from a wide range of provisions. I envision constitutional development to proceed most logically as follows:

First, the U.S. President would officially invite Israel and Palestine to submit draft constitutions as petitions for U.S. statehood. At the urging of the U.S. President, this invitation would be reiterated in a Congressional Resolution and be promoted by the State Department.

Second, Israeli and Palestinian government authorities would respond to the invitation by conducting two parallel activities: (a) engaging in a year-long national debate over the pros and cons of U.S. statehood, culminating in popular referenda, and (b) undertaking a year-long state constitution drafting exercise to identify sticking points and thorny issues. As part of the state constitution drafting exercise, a tripartite Israeli-Palestinian-U.S. Congressional Commission could provide ongoing guidance where constitutional provisions were problematic.

Finally, assuming favorable public opinion in Israel and Palestine, their legislatures and chief executives would submit the well-coordinated statehood constitutions to the U.S. Congress for approval. Following the process outlined above, there would be no surprises and the statehood vote would go quite smoothly.

---

6. A key to the U.S. Constitution's longevity is its flexibility. As Justice Thurgood Marshall once said, "For a sense of the evolving nature of the Constitution, we need look no further than the first three words of the document's preamble: 'We the People.' When the founding fathers used this phrase in 1787, they did not have in mind the majority of America's citizens...[They could not have imagined] that the document they were drafting would one day be construed by a Supreme Court to which had been appointed a woman and the descendant of an African slave."

Flags

Flags are important. They communicate volumes at a single glance. The change to the American flag is preordained: two more white stars in the blue upper left-hand corner. Graphical arts experts will determine which pattern works best with fifty-two stars. How about the Israeli and Palestinian flags?

I believe it would be wrong to require Israel and Palestine to make any change in their flags in order to join the United States. In a similar vein, the U.S. Supreme Court in 1911 ruled that Congress could not admit Oklahoma as a state subject to a condition concerning the location of its state capital. The Supreme Court said that part of state equality was an absence of conditions that apply to some but not other states. Since Congress never passed judgment on any other state's flag, it would be inappropriate for it to pass judgment on Israeli and Palestinian flags.

It may be observed that while the Palestinian flag[7] appears to be wholly secular, the Israeli flag appears blatantly religious, with its large blue Star of David. Does this not conflict with America's prohibition against state religion? Absolutely not.

The six-pointed Star of David is a symbol of the Jewish people. As such, it is a secular symbol that gets infused by most people with religious significance. Similarly, a Christmas tree can mean "winter holidays" to some while others may identify it with the Christian holy day. A crescent moon can conjure up astronomical thoughts or remind one of Islamic prayers. The point is that the meanings of symbols are the meanings people give them.

There are some symbols, such as the swastika, that trigger in most Western people odious and abhorrent feelings. Such symbols are appropriately absent from all U.S. state flags. But symbols that elicit positive emotions, even if they have double meanings in the realm of religion, should not be banned.

There are many Palestinians for whom the Israeli flag causes painful memories. Similarly, many Israelis could not stomach a Palestinian flag on their living-room wall. But these individualized reactions are not reasons to prohibit use of a symbol that is overwhelmingly welcomed in its own state. Even almost 150 years after the U.S. Civil War, hints of the confederate symbol in the flags of certain southern states unnerve some Northerners—and uplift some Southerners.

The Star of David imbues in most Israelis a sense of great pride in their survival despite overwhelming odds. There is no suggestion of state religion here, no prescriptions for worship. The Star of David is simply another way of saying, "Don't tread on me." It has a rightful place amongst the other fifty-one state flags of the expanded republic.

---

7. A Palestinian flag was first officially adopted in September 1948 at a Palestine National Council meeting in Gaza. It was the flag of a 1916 Arab Revolt.

Language

Nowhere in the U.S. Constitution does it say that English is the language of the land. Nevertheless, it often seems that way. Virtually all government proceedings are conducted in English. Spanish and other languages have a growing presence in the media, in government applications, in signage, and public health settings. English-only advocates occasionally speak up when primary schools teach children in a parental non-English tongue, or when they feel they are sinking below a rising polyglot tide.

Herzl was not concerned about the national language of Israel. He did not expect the rebirth of Hebrew. His practical bent led him to predict that whichever language was most used would become the national language. He pointed to Switzerland as proof that a single language is unnecessary to the success of a vibrant country.

Americans have good cause to want all U.S. citizens to speak English. A common tongue is an important part of a unified country. On the other hand, wanting all U.S. citizens to speak English is not the same thing as demanding that *only* English be spoken. The latter demand reduces freedom of thought and expression and diminishes cultural diversity. The fact that Hebrew in Israel and Arabic in Palestine are the predominant languages is irrelevant to American citizenship so long as English is *also* universally spoken.

It is reasonable to require that the official versions of each state's Constitution be in English and that all government business be transacted in parallel English/Hebrew for Israel and English/Arabic for Palestine. The official version of the Constitution needs to be in English because the English-speaking U.S. Supreme Court will need to interpret it from time to time. Bilingual government business is a wise idea because no one feels left out. There are of course additional costs with bilingual processes, but these costs are worth the benefits.

It would not be sensible for the rest of the United States to offer government or other services in Hebrew or Arabic. There are too few Hebrew-only and Arabic-only speakers outside of Israel and Palestine to justify this expense. Furthermore, most Palestinians and Israelis do understand English. Also, America's claim to fame as an immigrant nation means that there are far too many languages spoken to practically offer all of them as official parallel linguistic channels. Parallel language services make sense only in those localities where speakers of only a particular non-English language are concentrated. Examples include California's Little Vietnam, New York's Chinatown, Spanish-speaking parts of Texas and, hopefully soon, Israel and Palestine.

America is now a country of minorities. English is our lingua franca. English itself is changing all the time, morphing to the beat of each new wave of immigration. It would make us no less American to add in 6 million Israelis and 3 million

Palestinians, most of whom are bilingual.[8] Indeed, each decade America absorbs approximately this number of Latin American and Asian immigrants, the vast majority of whom speak less English than do typical Israelis and Palestinians. Within a generation or two, virtually all of the immigrants' offspring will be speaking English. Clearly, then, the status of English as the second language of Israelis and Palestinians is no reason to hold up their integration. Indeed, our language is likely to be enriched by many of the beautiful phrases of these ancient tongues.

Capitals

Let us be frank: neither Israelis nor Palestinians will ever settle, long term, for any capital but Jerusalem. At the time of this writing, the Palestinian capital is Ramallah, but that is only because the Israelis steadfastly refuse to give up sovereignty over any part of Jerusalem.[9] The Two Stars Plan is the only practical approach to permitting both Israel and Palestine to have their capitals in Jerusalem.

In 1948, at Israel's founding, there was an Old City Jerusalem in the east and newer developments in the west. While the UN Partition envisioned an internationalized single city, the 1949 Armistice line gave West Jerusalem to Israel and East Jerusalem to Jordan. A demilitarized zone around Mount Scopus and a set of buffer zones were also delineated.

West Jerusalem became a new town, built by the Israelis into a modern metropolis. Almost all of the Islamic, Christian, and Jewish holy sites are in East Jerusalem, and Jordan severely restricted access to the Jewish holy sites. During the 1967 War, the Israelis won control of East Jerusalem, mostly by house-to-house, hand-to-hand combat. Since that time, the physical plants and administration of East and West Jerusalem have become increasingly integrated.

The return to the pre-1967 borders called for in the Two Stars Plan means that Jerusalem will once again become two cities: East and West Jerusalem. However, all that was once problematic now becomes tractable. There would be no border crossings, red lines, green lines, fences, walls, or any other obstructions between the two halves of the city. Article 4, section 2 of the U.S.

8. English is the second language of both Israel and Palestine and is required in secondary and higher levels of education. Approximately 90% of Israelis speak English, as do a majority of Palestinians. Many Palestinians are trilingual, as they must know English, Hebrew, and Arabic in order to succeed in most business or professional endeavors.
9. Palestinians first formally adopted Jerusalem as their capital when they declared their independence in September 1948 at a Palestine National Council meeting in Gaza. This was recognized only by Egypt and the Arab League, while Jordan sponsored a larger Palestinian Congress meeting that favored Palestine's incorporation into Jordan.

Constitution says that "citizens of each state shall be entitled to all privileges and immunities of citizens in the several states." This means that no state can interfere with the free movement of people and goods across state lines. It is for this reason that one is scarcely aware of driving from New York to New Jersey, or from Cincinnati, Ohio, to its suburbs in Covington, Kentucky, or from Philadelphia, Pennsylvania, to its bedrooms in Camden, New Jersey. Under the Two Stars Plan, nothing more than a sign would indicate that a person had passed from West to East Jerusalem, or vice versa. Most people would be too busy chatting on their cell phones to even notice the sign.

There is another reason no gates, turnstiles, fences, or other obstructions would impede passage between the East Jerusalem capital of Palestine and the West Jerusalem capital of Israel. Article 1, section 10 of the U.S. Constitution prohibits any state from regulating imports and exports. Hence, there is no legal basis for any U.S. state to control the flow of traffic into or out of its borders. While the Two Stars Plan recreates two cities from one Jerusalem, this is more a matter of form than of substance. There will be two mayors, two city councils, and two school districts. Numerous other municipal functions will be duplicated in the East and the West. But someone visiting Jerusalem would notice no difference from today—except for a great reduction in anti-terrorism security.

An important factor is that Israelis now own substantial property in East Jerusalem, especially around the Jewish holy sites. Article 1, section 10 of the U.S. Constitution prohibits states from voiding contracts or revoking land grants after the fact. Hence, even while East Jerusalem serves as the capital of the U.S. state of Palestine, Jews can be confident of the continuation of Jewish-controlled shrines and of their residential housing along the ancient streets of the capital.

Jews living in Palestinian Jerusalem will, of course, be subject to Palestinian jurisdiction and taxation. Thus, the substantial Israeli development of East Jerusalem and the West Bank would actually enhance Palestine's tax base. However, to compensate for the loss of so much of Old Jerusalem to non-Palestinians, the demilitarized and no-man zones of the 1949 Armistice should fall within the borders of the new American state of Palestine.

The Two Stars Plan allows Israelis to retain sovereignty over Jerusalem, via their membership in the United States. At the same time, the plan also enables Palestinians to achieve sovereignty over Jerusalem, also via their membership in the United States. No other Middle East Plan provides a practical means of satisfying both Israeli and Palestinian insistence upon having Jerusalem as their capital.

De-Militarization and Nuclear Issues

The U.S. does not permit its states to retain standing armies.[10] Israel, by necessity, developed a huge army, so any solution to the Middle-East crisis will have to address the destiny of this force. The answer is straightforward: the Israeli Defense Forces (IDF) will be re-commissioned as Israel-based divisions of the U.S. National Guard, as well as into the appropriate divisions of the U.S. Armed Forces.

Recommissioning provides Israel with comfort that by joining with the United States it is not giving up a crucial asset, its national defense force, which has taken decades to establish. The only difference is that the control of this force will have shifted from the Israeli to the American government. Another benefit is that the Israeli economy will blossom after being largely relieved of the huge burden of supporting its very expensive military, which now consumes over one-tenth of its people's taxes.

Further economic gains will be realized from keeping most Israeli youngsters in the workforce instead of losing them during their mandatory enlistment years. The all-volunteer U.S. National Guard, Army, Navy, Air Force, and Marines will be open to all Israelis and Palestinians. However, since there is a 300-million-person American population to draw upon for voluntary enlistment, there will no longer be a need to have an Israeli draft to support its military.

Integration of the Israeli Defense Force (IDF) with the U.S. military establishment also provides more career development opportunities for Israeli defense professionals. Highly skilled Israeli officers are likely to rise rapidly within the much larger U.S. Armed Forces.

There will also be regrets that accompany the merging of the IDF into its U.S. counterpart. The IDF performs a vital nation-building role in Israel. It helps to acclimate immigrants to the Israeli culture. Indeed, as of 2003, immigrants comprised almost twice the percentage of army recruits as they represent in the overall population. This occurred because an increasing number of native-born Israelis are taking advantage of various exemptions to avoid the universal obligation (for non-Arab males) of three years of active duty, followed by one month a year in the reserves (until middle age).

It is generally speculated that the reason for the ever-dropping percentage of eligible adults that complete IDF service is that the West Bank patrols, now a major focus of the IDF, are very unpleasant. In essence, by controlling Palestinian

---

10. Article 1, section 10 of the U.S. Constitution forbids states from keeping troops or military vessels or engaging in war, "unless actually invaded, or in such imminent danger as will not admit of delay."

civilians, the IDF offers a rather negative sort of socialization, an "us versus them" indoctrination that many Israelis would rather avoid.

There are two ways to mitigate the loss of the IDF as a socializing institution. The first, as mentioned above, is to transform much of the IDF into Israel-based U.S. National Guard divisions. These are the modest state-based emergency-reserve forces envisioned in the Second Amendment to the U.S. Constitution. For reasons that modern-day Israelis could well identify with, such as close-at-hand security, tradition, and manhood training, several of the original thirteen colonies that formed the United States balked at losing their territorial militia entirely. They insisted upon the Second Amendment to the Constitution, which permitted a state-based National Guard on the condition that those locally-based forces would always be available to the national army. The purpose of the National Guard in the U.S. is mostly one of emergency relief, although it does include military training. Israeli National Guard recruiters could target their advertising to immigrants and identify the Israeli acculturation benefits of enlistment.

A second way to continue the IDF, though in a much-reduced form, would be as Israel-based divisions of the U.S. Army, Navy, and Air Force Reserves. This recognizes that "adulthood-training" and "acculturation" also occur within the U.S. Armed Forces. There, soldiers matriculate into a culture that is a discipline-oriented American mélange. This is as big an eye-opener for inner-city, rural, or new-immigrant American youth, as is the IDF for Ethiopian and Russian immigrants to Israel. As new members of the United States, it is as important that young Israelis, especially immigrants or their young adult children, be acculturated into the American way of life, as it is for them now to adjust to the Israeli culture.

Israeli and Palestinian youth can achieve both local and American acculturation benefits by enlisting in the U.S. Army, and then serving for several years (on long weekends once or twice a month) in the U.S. Army Reserves after their initial tour of duty ends. Service in the Reserves would take place close to a person's home. For example, Israel-based branches of the Reserves could provide continuing Israeli-accented acculturation assistance to young men and women after a couple of years of American-accented training in the active Army or Navy. Yet another option is for young people to enlist directly in the U.S. Army, Navy, or Air Force Reserves, thereby by-passing service in the continental United States entirely.

An important final issue to discuss under demilitarization is the question of Israel's nuclear arsenal. Upon accession to statehood, this arsenal would become part of America's cache and would be declared and possibly dismantled in accordance with the strategic-arms agreements. Israel will naturally feel very nervous about this step. She views nuclear arms as a guarantee of her survival and independence.

There is an old Zen saying that applies here: "Hold on tightly, let go lightly." While Israel stood alone, who could blame her for holding on with a fierce tightness to the only absolute assurance of security that the world has known? If nuclear arms were not such an assurance, then why did the U.S., Russia, China, France, and the U.K. insist on having them in their arsenals? However, as part of the United States, Israel will never again stand alone.

Israel will have as much stake in the U.S. nuclear arsenal as do the peoples of New Hampshire and Oregon. Neither of these states have nuclear-weapon silos within their borders. Yet, the peoples of both states still know that the bombs kept warm under concrete shelters in North Dakota and in prowling submarines provide their enemies with just as much nuclear deterrence.

With the guarantee of American nuclear protection, Israel can "let go lightly" of her nuclear arms, or at least transfer them to U.S. governmental control. In so doing, the cause of nuclear non-proliferation will also be advanced. The world will be one nation closer to its goal of a fingers-on-one-hand club of nuclear-equipped countries. That club can then practically continue its efforts—led by Russia and the United States—of dismantling those terrible weapons once and for all.

Currency Exchange

American states are not permitted to print their own currency. So what becomes of the Israeli shekel? How can one fairly grapple with the grab bag of dinars, pounds, dollars, and shekels that Palestinians shuffle through today? Fortunately, Europe has paved the way. If several European countries could fairly exchange their liras, pesetas, francs, and even almighty marks for Euros, certainly the Israelis and Palestinians can trade in their tired bills for U.S. dollars.

The dollar-swap will be especially beneficial for the Palestinian people, who have no single currency. They lose great amounts of money each year in exchange-rate fluctuations, broker's fees, and inflation. The Israelis will benefit hugely as well. The U.S. dollar is much less prone to inflation than the shekel. Also, wealthier Israelis will no longer fear the legal or moral consequences of holding their cash in off-shore, non-shekel accounts.

The U.S. economy can easily handle the extra currency obligations of Israel and Palestine. As of 2003, the Israeli economy generated less than $100 billion worth of income, which is about 1% the size of the U.S. economy. This is not surprising, since the Israeli population is but 2% of the U.S. population, and it is a commensurably productive country. The Palestinian economy is much smaller than the Israeli economy. Hence, even if all transactions were accomplished in cash (a less frequent mode of exchange in Israel than in the U.S.), a modest 1% increase in U.S. currency circulation would easily cover the needs of the Two Stars Plan.

Lawsuits

It has been over fifty years since America's last two states, Alaska and Hawaii, joined the union. Those states were rather undeveloped. The other thirty-five states that joined the original thirteen were annexed when they too were rather undeveloped. Almost all of the states joined during the nineteenth century. Society was very much less litigious in those days. The legal profession was young and commercial disputes were simpler. Some believe today's litigiousness arises from a mindset of "fault and blame." Instead of people being accountable for their own actions and inactions, they seek to place blame.

The concept of human accountability arose largely from the monotheistic faiths practiced by the majority of Israelis and Palestinians. Prior to monotheism, misfortune was attributed to the actions of a god. Humans could be blamed for not satisfying a god, but the dissatisfaction was rooted in the provision of temples, idols, and sacrifices in their god's honor. There was no connection between a person's day-to-day actions toward another person and the consequences of those actions.

As a teenager, Abraham was asked to watch his father's idol shop for an afternoon. When his father returned home he was outraged to see that all of the idols had been smashed, except for a large club-wielding statue. "What the hell happened here?" his father roared in anger, seeing financial ruin in the crumbled rock and rubble that littered the floor.

Prescient Abraham, who had tired of losing arguments with his father on the subject of monotheism, replied, "The large idol with the club smashed all of the other ones."

Flushed with too much anger to think first, the father yelled, "You idiot. These are just made of wood and clay; they can't do anything!"

One can imagine the smile that must have rolled across young Abraham's face as he calmly replied, "That is what I've been saying all along."

In the Christian, Islamic, and Jewish faiths that Abraham spawned, there is but one God, and this God wants no idols or human sacrifices. Instead, people behaving responsibly toward each other satisfy this one all-powerful God. Monotheism ushered in the notion of brotherhood by shifting the focus of fault from a god to each person and by shifting the focus of good behavior from sacrifices to relations among people. It is high time for this concept of brotherhood to extend itself to our judicial system. People must take personal responsibility for an adverse turn of affairs rather than seeking resolution or retribution via litigation.

Even with a much greater degree of personal accountability, there will still be a need for Israelis and Palestinians to settle disputes legally, both amongst and between their ethnic groups. In the American system, states have considerable latitude to develop their own courts, laws, and legal precedents. The principal limitations are that their laws must be consistent with their state constitutions and must not tran-scend certain basic legal principles contained in the U.S. Constitution.[11] In addi-tion, if a dispute arises between residents of two different states, or if a federal constitutional issue is involved, the dispute may be handled under the U.S. federal legal system.

For example, suppose two Israelis are suing each other prior to the annexation of Israel as an American state. That lawsuit would proceed unaffected and would be settled in an Israeli court under Israeli law. On the other hand, suppose a Palestinian living in today's West Bank sues an Israeli living in Israel. That lawsuit could be removed to a federal U.S. court because it would be a lawsuit involving residents of two different American states, Israel and Palestine. Finally, suppose a Palestinian living in today's West Bank sues a West Bank Israeli settler in an Israeli court, under Israeli law. That lawsuit might be removed to a Palestinian court, since both parties would be subject to Palestinian jurisdiction. The Palestinian court, however, would need to resolve the matter under Israeli law, as there would not yet be a body of Palestinian law at the time of the alleged wrong. *Ex post facto* laws, which make something illegal after it already occurred, are specifically pro-scribed in the U.S. Constitution.

For all of the above examples, as well as numerous other permutations, it is important to remember that obligations or contracts entered into before state-hood occurs must continue to be respected. If they were not, an aggrieved party could appeal an adverse decision to the federal court system. Bases for appeal to the U.S. federal judicial system also include cases of legal prejudice because a liti-gant is either Israeli or Palestinian, as this could violate the Constitutional guar-antees known as "due process" and "equal protection."[12]

---

11. For example, it would not work for the Palestinian Constitution to say, "Shari'a is the law of this state," as that would cross the line of impermissible state promotion of reli-gion. On the other hand, there would be no problem with the Palestinian legislature adopting as its state criminal and civil law, pursuant to a secular constitution, many, if not most, of the specific prescriptions and proscriptions provided in Shari'a. All that needs to be excluded are those provisions that transcend due process, equal protec-tion, or other basic U.S. constitutional protections, which are intended to permit people of diverse faiths and beliefs to live together in peace.

12. Article 3, section 2 of the U.S. Constitution authorizes federal judicial courts to get involved in any matter that arises "under this Constitution" [such as due process or equal protection issues] as well as "Controversies between two or more States; between a State and Citizens of another State; between Citizens of different States; between Citizens of the same State claiming Lands under Grants of different States, and between a State, or the Citizens thereof, and foreign States, Citizens or Subjects."

It should also be kept in mind that the President nominates federal judges in the U.S. and the Senate approves them. While it is likely that the lowest level of federal judges (known as District Court judges) in each of Israel and Palestine will, at least initially, be of Israeli and Palestinian backgrounds respectively, this is not required under the Constitution. The U.S. does not apportion judges by demographics. As one moves up the judicial ladder, to Courts of Appeal and ulti-mately to the U.S. Supreme Court, judges of non-Israeli or Palestinian descent will inevitably decide legal matters involving Israelis and Palestinians.

In summary, in the vast majority of their affairs, even as part of the United States, people living in Israel will be governed by Israeli law adopted by an Israeli legislature and interpreted by Israeli state judges. Similarly, people living in Palestine will be governed by a brand-new set of Palestinian laws adopted by a newly-elected Palestinian legislature and interpreted under a newly-created Palestinian court system. Even when the law permits a dispute to be removed to a federal court, the federal judge will apply either Israeli or Palestinian law, if appropriate. Consequently, by joining with the United States, Israelis and Palestinians would be giving up very little control over their daily lives. It is mostly in the realm of ensuring certain minimal civil rights, or in the interests of ensuring fairness in litigation between residents of different states, that federal courts will apply constitutional or common-law principles. These instances cer-tainly serve the best interests of the Israeli and Palestinian people as they do of all people who come within their jurisdiction.

Civil Rights

Israel has a good civil-rights track record for a country that is essentially in the midst of a civil war. Many people criticize Israeli treatment of Palestinian detainees. Few if any countries have a better record with the residents of a rebel-lious province. Palestine is not a province of Israel, and the "Israeli-Palestinian space" does not actually constitute a country. Hence, legally speaking, there is not a civil war going on. Instead, what we see on television is the rough-and-tough administration of an adjacent proto-country. But these formalities gloss over the reality: much of a largely integrated socioeconomic unit, the Israeli-Palestinian space, is in a state of rebellion. No country deals kindly with such situations. The United States suspended habeas corpus during its Civil War. Remember Biafra? How about Chechnya? Or Northern Ireland?

The beauty of the Two Stars Plan is that it ends both the civil-rights abuses and the rebellion, and it does so with both justice and security. The de facto civil war will be over. Both Israel and Palestine will be respected states of the United States. The need for extreme measures will have ended. Consequently, Israel and

Palestine must respect the civil rights of their residents, and other Americans, no less than the state of Florida must respect the civil rights of both its residents and the snowbirds from the North.

Neither Israel nor Palestine will be able to offer, nor permit, private entities serving the public to offer preferential treatment based on religion or ethnic background. For example, while the military draft will be over, the Israeli National Guard must be as open to Israeli Arabs as to non-Arabs. In another vein, a housing development in Palestine must be as open to Jewish purchasers as to non-Jewish purchasers.

Civil rights include the duty of governments to treat people as individuals rather than as members of an ethnic, religious, or sexual class. For example, Arabs, whether they are Israeli or Palestinian residents, cannot be forced to endure different security measures than Jews. Neither Palestinian nor Israeli officials can fail to recognize inter-marriages. In some views, such as those prevalent in Canada, Scandinavia, and the State of Vermont, civil rights include the right of marriage between two men or two women.

The boundary of civil rights constantly evolves along with societal consensus. It is for this reason that states in America have great latitude in setting this boundary. It is only required that fundamental fairness prevails, that similar situations are treated similarly, and that specific constitutional rights are respected. Those rights can be summarized as freedom *of* expression, religion, and thought; freedom *from* unreasonable search, seizure, and punishment; and the *rights to* a fair jury trial, a zone of personal privacy, voting, and unrestricted travel.[13]

With the adoption of U.S. statehood there are many detainees in Israeli and Palestinian jails that will have to be released. Unless a detainee can be proved to have broken a valid law, based on legitimate police work and a fair trial, he or she must be released. It should be emphasized though, that these rights apply to Israeli and Palestinian citizens, who will all become U.S. citizens. An outside provocateur who is not an Israeli or Palestinian citizen, and hence not a U.S. citizen, may be detained differently.

---

13. Some of these rights and freedoms were clearly expressed in the Constitution, while others were interpreted over the last 200 years. The concept of enumerated powers is expressed clearly in the 9th Amendment to the Constitution: the enumeration of certain rights "shall not be construed to deny or disparage others retained by the people." Similarly, the 10th Amendment says, "Powers not delegated to the United States by the Constitution, nor prohibited by it to the States, are reserved to the States respectively, or to the people." These two amendments clearly preclude any conflict between the secular Constitution and the holy books of Christianity, Islam, and Judaism. *Expresio unius est exclusio alterius:* to express or include one thing implies the exclusion of the other, or of the alternative.

Both Israelis and Palestinians need to forgive each other for breaches of civil rights and civil behavior that have occurred during the past several decades. Both need to recognize that during emergency situations, when there is fighting for freedom or for security, the first victim is civility. Nevertheless, despite the outrages of exploded civilians and stolen lives, a remarkable undercurrent of Israeli-Palestinian brotherhood always existed. Transplantable organs passed between Palestinians and Israelis. Countless kindnesses transpired that never made it to the headlines.

Americans recognize that the civil rights prescribed by the U.S. Constitution ultimately evolved from the divine principles of brotherhood that were birthed in the Holy Land. Hence, as peaceful states of the United States, Israel and Palestine will certainly fit within U.S. civil-rights protections. Americans, on the other hand, can rest assured that the peoples of their two new states know the meaning of civil rights deep down in their ancestral souls.

Health Care and Social Costs

Many things in life are desirable, but just not affordable. Geopolitics is no different. The next reasonable question to ask is whether or not the U.S. can afford the costs of absorbing 10 million more people, and two more states, at a time of great federal budget pressure. Germany's economy has reeled for more than a decade due to the huge social welfare expenditures associated with absorbing East Germany.

Health care and education represent the large majority of government-payable costs associated with the absorption of immigrants. Since a country sets minimum standards for health care and education, new immigrants will immediately be entitled to these services but will not have had a chance to financially contribute to their costs. Over time, the taxes paid by immigrants will cover their health care and social costs, but let us assume that the entire burden has to be shouldered by the federal government for ten years.

Starting with health care, the United States pays approximately $6,000 per person per year in Medicare costs. About 20% of the U.S. population relies on this system in lieu of self-paid private health insurance (principally, the elderly and disabled). Were the same percentage of the Israeli and Palestinian populations enrolled in this system, a "region of magnitude" estimate of the increased burden of the Two Stars Plan would be $12 billion per year—a 2%–3% increase over current outlays. Because the Medicare system is already in financial trouble it would be reasonable for Congress to authorize a special Two Stars for Peace allocation. This special allocation could be calculated to decline each year and sunset in ten years as Medicare taxes from Israel and Palestine grow to cover their share of the system's costs.

In addition to Medicare, all U.S. citizens that meet certain near-poverty defi-
nitions are entitled to health-care benefits via a state-administered system known
as Medicaid. As a *high-end* assumption, let us presume that the federally-paid
portion of Medicaid payments would be comparable to one-half current
Medicare payment levels, and that 80% of Palestinians and 20% of Israelis would
qualify for them.[14] In this case, the Two Stars for Peace budget allocation would
need to grow by an additional $12 billion (4 million people times $3000/per-
son/year). As of 2001, the U.S. was spending about $280 billion on Medicaid,
hence the Two Stars for Peace plan might require, based on high-end assumptions, an annual Medicaid budget increase of up to 4%. The higher Medicaid-
qualified percentage of the population, as compared to the two states' percentage
of the total American population, represents the impoverishment that has fallen
upon the Palestinian people as a result of decades of statelessness.

The major remaining federal social expenditures would be old-age pensions—
called social security—and education. The social security-system should be
budget neutral because payments into it during one's working life are offset by
payments out of it upon retirement. Social security is in the headlines these days
because projections show it going bankrupt due to people living longer than
anticipated. What will be the effect of adding a couple of million Israeli and
Palestinian retirees who never made a contribution into the system?

There are two reasons why the Israeli and Palestinian impact upon social security will be *de minimis* in the near-term, and either neutral or positive in the mid-
to-long term. As for the Palestinians, they have an average age of seventeen, about
half the U.S. average. Thus only a very small proportion of their population has
reached the social-security entitlement age of sixty-five. However, by adding millions of young Palestinian social security taxpayers to the system over the next
several years, the system will receive an unexpected, positive boost.

Israel, on the other hand, has a well-developed and solvent social-security system of its own, pursuant to its 1954 National Insurance Law. Actuarial and legal
experts could work out arrangements whereby Israeli residents maintained access
to their existing pension system in lieu of U.S. social security, or simply merged
the two systems. Since the Israeli system is solvent, a merger of the two systems
would not create any net burden on the U.S. system.

U.S. federal government spending on education, welfare, and related training
programs amounts to less than $700/person/year. Applied to the Israeli and
Palestinian populations, this spending rate translates into a need for $7 billion of
additional spending. Compared to the existing $200 billion of spending in the

---

14. Palestinian per capita income is estimated at $2000-$3000, approximately one-sixth
    or less of the levels in Israel, which in turn are about one-half of U.S. levels.

federal budget for these matters, the Two Stars for Peace plan increases the budget by a mere 3.5%.

All totaled, our estimates of the U.S. federal budget cost of the Two Stars for Peace plan is in the range of $31 billion per year, representing $12 billion for Medicare, $12 billion for Medicaid, and $7 billion for education and welfare. On the other hand, the federal government tax revenues will increase through the annexation of Israel and Palestine. In the U.S., federal tax revenues represent approximately 20% of GDP. Applying that same percentage to Israel's GDP, and expecting (initially) no material tax revenue contribution from Palestine, the U.S. can expect that about $22 billion per year of the estimated $31 billion annual cost of the Two Stars plan will be offset with tax revenues. Consequently, the net cost of the Two Stars Plan is about $9 billion a year initially, and decreasing rapidly as Palestine and Israel integrate into the U.S. economy.

We are in a reasonable range. The $9-billion-a-year initial cost of the Two Stars plan represents only about 0.5% of the federal government's budget. The country can lose much more than that amount from world instability associated with the Middle-East crisis. Experts are invited to refine these numbers with comprehensive computer models. But the estimates in this book cannot be off by more than a factor of two, either on the high or the low end. Any costs within this range are indisputably affordable by the U.S. I also assert that the benefits of lasting peace in the Middle East are well worth this price. Finally, weaving the synergistic strengths and energies of the Israeli and Palestinian people into the American fabric will generate a return on investment that no rational person should refuse.

Foreign Affairs and Rights of Return

Both the Israelis and Palestinians are very outward-looking peoples. For both of them it has largely been a matter of necessity—more than half of the Jews entitled by Israeli law to claim citizenship live outside of Israel, and more than half of all Palestinians live outside the Israeli-Palestinian space. Consequently, both peoples have worked hard to develop foreign relations. What will happen to these embassies, consulates, and representative offices after American statehood? What disposition can the Two Stars Plan make for the millions of Jews who may want to emigrate to Israel and the millions of Palestinians who may long to return home?

The U.S. Constitution wisely forbids states from entering into foreign treaties. It also, in article 4, takes upon the United States the obligations of treaties entered into previously by the new states. The logical conclusion is that the foreign agreements of both Israel and Palestine become the foreign agreements of the United States proper. In a similar vein, when two companies merge, each of their previous contracts become the contracts of the new merged company. Sometimes revolutionary countries disavow the agreements of predecessor governments, but usually they are respected and wound down if they were disadvantageous.

Embassies and foreign-representation offices that Israel and the Palestinian Authority have established overseas can be transformed into trade offices to encourage investment in or tourism to the new states. Members of the Israeli and Palestinian diplomatic corps will find their talents welcomed within the U.S. State Department as well as in the business world. Under the peace and security of the Two Stars Plan, a renaissance of worldwide business interest in Israel and Palestine can be expected.

The interests of Israel and Palestine in providing a "right of return" for their co-ethnicists presents both a problem as well as a solution. The Israelis rank their Right of Return Law as important as their Basic Laws, or de facto constitution. It is considered a fundamental law, even a raison d'être for Israel's existence. The Palestinians can point to well over a million refugee brethren suffering through life in Jordanian, Lebanese, and Syrian refugee camps. How can it be fair to include those inside the West Bank as U.S. citizens but to exclude those who, mostly due to chance, ended up on the other side of the Jordan River?

The problem arises from the fact that long ago states lost their authority to decide matters of immigration and citizenship. It would be impossible for Israel and Palestine, as American states, to be given the authority to admit new citizens or exclude newly-admitted citizens from taking up residency in their states. To be clear, once Israel and Palestine become American states, there will no longer be passport controls between those states and the other fifty states. Travel from Israel or Palestine to Pennsylvania or South Carolina will be as transparent as travel today from Rhode Island or West Virginia to Iowa or Tennessee.

Initially, American states did have some immigration and citizenship-granting authority, even though article 1, section 8 of the U.S. Constitution gave Congress the power to establish uniform naturalization rules. Some states used their authority to admit large numbers of African-American slaves, none of whom were ever given citizenship. Some of these states also used their authority to deny citizenship even to freed slaves. Section 1 of the 14th Amendment to the U.S. Constitution resolved the question of who, at minimum, was a U.S. citizen: "All persons born or naturalized in the United States, and subject to the jurisdiction thereof, are citizens of the United States and of the State wherein they reside." Today, immigration and naturalization is wholly under federal control. Hence, by acts of Congress, additional groups of people can be considered naturalized citizens.

When new states join America, their residents immediately become U.S. citizens by virtue of the fact that they have been admitted to the Union on an equal basis with all other states. Now, let's apply this law and history to the Right of

Return issue. A straightforward case can be made that Palestinians who can prove they were born in Israel or Palestine, as well as their descendants and their immediate family members, would be U.S. citizens, even if they are currently residing in a refugee camp outside of Israeli-Palestinian space. Their situations are different from passport-bearing Israelis or Palestinians only by virtue of their current residence, which is unavoidably displaced due to the long civil war. Their situations are also consistent with the touchstone for U.S. citizenship, namely, birth in an American state.

A different solution is needed for the remaining people in Diaspora, such as second-degree relatives of Palestinian refugees or Russian Jews. Congress could pass legislation that provides an adequate number of "territorial return" or "territorial reunion" visa slots each year for persons who want to settle in Israel or Palestine. When it comes time to upgrade their visas to permanent residency or full citizenship, such individuals would have to prove that they did in fact settle in Israel or Palestine. Similarly, when someone comes to the United States under a fiancée visa, they will not be permitted to advance to permanent residency unless they prove that they are in fact married to an American citizen. With regard to the "territorial return" visas for Israel and Palestine, it would probably not be legal to restrict them to Jews and Palestinians, respectively. On the other hand, those are the majority of people who would avail themselves of such an opportunity.[15] Visa applications could also require a compelling reason for territorial return, such as ancestral ties to the land.

The Right of Return issue is well managed by the Two Stars Plan. Nearly all Palestinians may be deemed U.S. citizens outright, by virtue of their parents' or grandparents' birth on what will now be American-Palestinian or American-Israeli soil. Existing laws can accommodate their close relatives without difficulty. Others, including Jews that want to immigrate to Israel from Russia, can be accommodated by a modest amendment to existing U.S. immigration law. This small change would open up an adequate number of "territorial return" settlement visas that can mature into full citizenship once the individual fulfills the normal and customary obligations.

Americans need not worry about the number of "Right of Return" immigrants overwhelming the budgetary calculations provided under the section on Health Care and Social Costs. The U.S. currently absorbs approximately one million immigrants a year, and ten percent of its population is foreign born. It is

---

15. Most people using Israel's Right of Return law today do not have a Jewish mother, which is the religious definition of a Jew. More than a third of the "returnees" today do not even have a Jewish father, but are only one-quarter Jewish, based on a grandparent, or not Jewish at all, in the case of a "returnee's" immediate family.

not realistic that all remaining Jews in the world, or all overseas Palestinians, will immigrate upon statehood. After all, the Jews have been free to immigrate to Israel for decades, and their numbers average 70,000 per year, mostly from Russia. There are only about 4–5 million Palestinians living overseas, including many in America. If their return to Palestine matched the rate at which the comparable number of overseas Jews have been returning to Israel, the total Right of Return visas would not exceed 140,000 annually, tapering to ever lower levels after a number of years. These modest figures are well within the penumbra of the healthcare and social cost estimations noted earlier.

Summary

This section of the book has shown that the Two Stars Plan is a practical solution to the ongoing problems of the Middle East. The Plan has been examined from each possible "show-stopper" standpoint and has been shown to stand tall in every case. The Two Stars Plan is flexible enough to accommodate returnees, affordable enough to provide American-level social services, and strong enough to manage demilitarization without sacrificing security. It provides both states with Jerusalem as a capital, respects the integrity of existing flags, and enables property rights to be settled fairly in accordance with well-developed legal precedents. Best of all, the Two Stars Plan enables Israelis and Palestinians to manage their day-to-day affairs in accordance with their own laws and justice system, subject only to the "safety net" of constitutional civil rights and a federal judiciary for cross-state or constitutional issues.

It may seem that with such a practical solution to a seemingly intractable problem, all persons of good will would stand up and pledge their allegiance to its most rapid possible implementation. Indeed, this is my sincere hope, as I'm confident that millions of lives will benefit thereby, most of all the lives of young Palestinians and Israelis. In politics, though, nothing comes easy, and in geopolitics, the status quo can be as hard as pre-Cambrian rock.

It is incumbent upon us then to look at the Two Stars Plan from every possible angle. Perhaps by rebutting all the reasonable objections to the Two Stars Plan we can shatter the rock-hard underpinnings of the status quo. By shining a light into the crevasses of belief, attitude, and value that support the status quo, we can perhaps highlight the hidden fears and worries that would make it difficult for people to adopt this new idea. So it is to this task that we now turn, commencing with important religious perspectives and then proceeding to nationalistic concerns of Americans, Israelis, and Palestinians.

3

In Respect of Religion

We must learn to live together as brothers or perish together as fools.

—Rev. Martin Luther King, speech in St. Louis, March 22, 1964

Our Constitution was made only for a moral and religious people. It is wholly inadequate to the government of any other.

—John Quincy Adams, Sixth President of the United States

Perhaps nowhere today is there a more obvious need for the correct use of political authority than in the dramatic situation of the Middle East and the Holy Land…The fratricidal struggle that daily convulses the Holy Land and brings into conflict the forces shaping the immediate future of the Middle East shows clearly the need for men and women who, out of conviction, will implement policies firmly based on the principle of respect for human dignity and human rights. Such policies are incomparably more advantageous to everyone than the continuation of conflict…Religion has a vital role in fostering gestures of peace and in consolidating conditions for peace. It exercises this role all the more effectively if it concentrates on what is proper to it: attention to God, the fostering of universal brotherhood, and the spreading of a culture of human solidarity.

—Pope John Paul II, January 1, 2003

Israeli-Palestinian space contains many of the holiest sites in Christianity, Islam, and Judaism. Sometimes, they are virtually the same site, such as Jerusalem's spiritual ground zero, known as the Temple Mount to Jews and the Noble Sanctuary to Muslims. For this reason alone, it is mandatory to propose a solution that specifically respects the views of these great religions. Additionally, to many, Israel *is* the *Jewish* state, and to others Palestine *should be* an *Islamic* state. Can these theocratic views be reconciled with statehood in secular America?

Christianity

Two billion Christians populate our world—about one-third of humanity. Many things are said and done in the name of Christianity. At the center of all these things is a belief in one God who wants all men and women to live in peace.

Christians realize that God cares as much for Muslims and Jews as for Christians. Just as all three religions worship the same God with all the obedience God demands, that same God must therefore look with equal kindness on the peoples of all three religions. God's love inspired Jesus to spread this message far and wide: love thy neighbor.

Everything in Christian thought directs one to solutions which further neighborly compassion and understanding. As demonstrated in Chapter 2, the outstanding feature of the Two Stars Plan is that it provides the most conducive environment to peace by far. Consequently, from the perspective of Christianity, the Two Stars Plan must be consistent with God's plan.

As a particular example, there are many holy Christian places in Israeli-Palestinian space. Foremost among these may be the birthplace of Jesus, in Bethlehem. But also very important are the places in Nazareth, Jerusalem, and other towns where Jesus or his disciples performed miracles. Under the status quo, access to these places is usually dangerous and sometimes impossible. The constant hail of gunfire around these places disrespects the very message Jesus brought to earth.

Even under the two-state roadmap to peace, the neighboring sovereignties would be duty-bound to arm themselves against their neighbors. Their fears would overshadow their will to adhere to God's mandate of peace. With two sovereign states, there would be border crossings and other socioeconomic divisions that would sap the energy of the land, much like the lead rods in an atomic reactor reduce power output. These divisions inevitably foster discrimination, which breeds anger and diminishes the human potential for love.

As two stars on the American flag, Israelis and Palestinians would live in neighborly peace. Christian shrines in the Holy Land will finally be as free of gunfire as are the thousands of churches that highlight America's urban and rural landscapes. For this alone, one could rest assured that Jesus and his ancient followers would bless the Two Stars Plan.

America is no heaven on earth, nor does it arrogantly presume to achieve such status. But America is a place where people of every religion are mandated by law to respect the religious practices of their neighbors. It is also a place where people are encouraged by policy to build diverse neighborly bonds. It is exactly this kind of environment that Jesus devoted his life to creating in the Holy Land. It honors every Christian to help bring it home.

Islam

Over one billion Muslims populate our world—about one out of every six people alive. Many things are said and done in the name of Islam. Rising high above all such words and deeds is the concept of obedience to one God.

Muslims realize that obedience to one God applies to all people, for all people are subject to God's control. Muslim thought particularly realizes that Jews and Christians are close to God, for the Koran recounts God's promises to Jewish and Christian prophets with the same respect it accords the Prophet Mohammed.

Jerusalem is the third holiest city in Islam, following Mecca and Medina. Furthermore, many places visited by Abraham, sites where he constructed shrines to God, exist throughout Israeli-Palestinian space and are special in Islam. Ibrahim, as he is known in the Koran, is as much the father of Muslims as he is the father of Jews, for he is as much the father of Ishmael as he is the father of Isaac. The two brothers, we are told in the Bible, came together to bury their father in a cave near Hebron. With so much religious heritage in tow, how can Islam not be vitally concerned with the sovereign status of Israeli-Palestinian space? How can that concern be most satisfactorily addressed?

Islam teaches the absolute supremacy of God over man. Hence, all man-made borders and sovereignties are superficial. King Hussein of Jordan, a lineal descendant of Mohammed, once said that conflict over Jerusalem should be resolved by considering it to be under the sovereignty of God. Indeed, if true for Jerusalem, it is also true for all Israeli-Palestinian space. In the ultimate sense, he is right, because God has absolute supremacy over lines in the sand drawn by mortals. But in the practical arena of everyday affairs, some temporal entity must be given administrative responsibility. It is much easier for everyone to worship God and obey his laws if societal infrastructure is managed prudently.

Thus, sovereignty for Muslims depends upon which way will administrative responsibility for God's Holy Land be most equitably and effectively discharged? There are three relevant possibilities: Israeli control (the status quo), bifurcated Israeli-Palestinian control (the two-state roadmap), or bifurcated Israeli-Palestinian control under American management (the Two Stars Plan).

The status quo has proven itself a disaster. Imagine how disappointed God would be, were he a landlord, to return back from a several-years sojourn and see his estate pockmarked with burning houses, bombed buildings, bullet holes, dashed dreams, and fallow fields. The status quo cannot possibly be considered a good way to manage God's Realm.

The two-state roadmap doesn't look too good either. It violates one of the main rules of good management: have a single entity accountable for a task. Having Israel and Palestine separately accountable for the management of different portions of an integral environmental and socioeconomic space is like asking two farmers to be in charge of what to plant on a small piece of land. It is a recipe for argument, procrastination, and low productivity. In the end, some crops may be grown, but much land will also be wasted. Common resources such as water or tools will always be flashpoints for a total managerial breakdown.

Who of us would entrust our backyard to two different people to manage? None of us who is wise, for sure. Surely we can do better for God's Holy Land than a solution of the two-state roadmap sort, which we would not adopt for our own property.

Finally, we are left to consider the Two Stars Plan. Does it meet Islam's demand that land under "God's sovereignty" be optimally managed? How good a job would America do as the "entity in charge," with Israel and Palestine delegated responsibility for non-conflicting areas of jurisdiction? Based on history, the answer is "a good job, carried out efficiently and equitably, with a light hand and a willingness to always improve."

It is undeniable that Americans are good managers. With just 5% of the world's population, they produce about one-third of the world's economic value. While she has her share of man-made wastelands, she has also managed to preserve for posterity vast tracts of nature, such as the Grand Canyon and redwood forests as old as the Koran. America also excels in guaranteeing visitors the experience they are seeking, be it a thrill at an entertainment park or reverie at a national park. American management techniques are task-specific, and in the realm of politics, it is only through the statehood process that America can maintain its status.

America's statehood system is actually a prudent method for managing widely-dispersed assets. While she had the opportunity to have many colonies, she had hardly any. Instead, America tends to incorporate new lands into her whole on a basis of equality and with great respect for local rights. While the components of the Soviet Union, England, and Spain couldn't wait to fly apart, the components of the United States continue to co-habit in peace. Consequently, by managing Israeli-Palestinian space via two new American states, Israel and Palestine, America is simply extending to the Middle East a system that has worked amazingly well for nearly a quarter of a thousand years.

America will not be the dreaded micromanager "who does it all himself," for most of the work will be reserved for the states of Israel and Palestine. To everyone's benefit, though, these states' powers will be defined in the Constitution so as to avoid conflict with each other and with the people they govern.

America is also not the hapless "absentee manager," for this would be no different from the two-state roadmap. The U.S. federal courts are vigilant in ensuring that states do not abridge civil rights or impede interstate commerce. The President of the United States is duty-bound to send in as many troops as it takes to enforce these decisions.

In business terms, America delegates neither too much nor too little, and her vibrant democracy enables her to correct her course as needed. This kind of management is tailor-made for the Holy Land. The Bible and Koran tell us that God gave Israeli-Palestinian space to *all* the seed of Abraham/Ibrahim. Today, this seed practices Islam as well as Judaism, Protestantism as well as Catholicism. Given these unique facts, the best management for this unique portion of God's domain is the federal-state plurality-friendly structure prescribed in the Two Stars Plan.

Islam is concerned that special places of holiness on earth fall under proper custody. Hence, all of *umma*, the world community of Islam, understandably concerns itself with today's situation in Israeli-Palestinian space. Islam helps us to remember that the only real sovereignty on earth is the one God who created it all. We humans are but caretakers of his sovereign lands. As such, we have an obligation to be excellent managers.

There are some who would like to see an Islamic state in Palestine. But this is not a solution that best implements the Koran. Ibrahim's seed is now many nations, as God predicted it would be, and each of these nations must feel welcome in the land promised to them collectively. The *principles* of Islam may still form the *backbone* of statutory law in an American state of Palestine. This is because the U.S. Constitution demands that considerable deference be shown to the local lawmaking authority of each of the American states. Hence, Palestine will assuredly be an Islamic-friendly state, while, at the same time, it remains a secular state to best accord with the intent of the Koran.

By prohibiting interference with religion, the U.S. Constitution places God above man. Hence, *jahiliyya*, or what some Islamists refer to as a "state of ignorance" due to the denial of God's supremacy, cannot exist in America. Consequently, a Palestinian state of America may be *Dar al-Islam* (an abode of Islam) without a theocratic political structure. Communism or fascism is *jahiliyya*. America is the antithesis of this because religious tolerance based on God's supremacy over man is what America is all about.

We must recognize that different lands call for different solutions respective of the unique historical, cultural, and geographical facts that prevail. The multiplicity of entitlements that prevail in Israeli-Palestinian space calls for a manager that respects religious diversity, local authority, and civil rights. Such a manager must also be strong enough to ensure that peace prevails. In today's world, there is no better candidate than the United States. Consequently, Islam's interests are protected by the Two Stars Plan.

Judaism

Nearly fifteen million Jews are alive today—about one-fourth of one percent of all human beings. Binding Jews together is a faith in a single God who looks after his people.

Jews realize that all people are God's people, for all people are of common descent. Jewish thought particularly realizes that God's people include Christians and Muslims, for these believers also descend from Abraham, as do the Jews.

It is often difficult for Jews to believe God really is looking after them. Jews have been chased out of Israel at least twice and murdered en masse in several European countries. On the other hand, each misfortune, no matter how terrible, somehow led to a higher level of existence. Their initial displacement to Babylon led to a memorializing of Jewish identity via the writing of a holy book, the Torah, or Old Testament. Even the horror of the Holocaust led to firm Western support for the establishment of Israel. God's promise can be seen in the fact that no religion has survived as long as Judaism, and Hebrew is the oldest language in general use.

Judaism teaches that the value of human life is more important than all other considerations. Given this teaching, as well as the Jews' ongoing fight for their own security, it is not surprising that the religion scrutinizes new developments in terms of their effect on Judaism's survival. Religious leaders ask themselves, "Is this development the hand of God watching over his people?" They challenge each other to disprove the hypothesis that some new plan, be it Herzl's *Judenstaat* or some new level of assimilation (loosening of tradition, intermarriage) is not actually the evil hand of treachery luring Jews away from the patient wait for a Messiah, or simply away from the safety of God's promise of protection.

Even the most conservative strains of Judaism should see that the Two Stars Plan is consistent with the Torah. For those who believe an independent state of Israel is premature because the Messiah has not yet arrived, the replacement of Israeli sovereignty with secular American authority must be viewed positively. For those who desire that Israel extend to its biblical borders of Judea and Samaria, the unification of all the lands west of the Jordan River under a single friendly sovereign should be viewed positively. And for those who long to live in the footsteps of patriarchs, including homesteading hilltops now full of Palestinian olive groves or village streets now steeped in Arab life, they may.

The days of arbitrarily bulldozing Palestinian life out of the way whenever a handful of zealots want to settle somewhere will be over. But this is nothing to regret, for it contradicted the biblical requirements of neighborliness and resulted in constant uncertainty and insecurity. These were not the acts of Judaism, but the acts of zealots who were willing to pay almost any price for the vivification of ancient script. Yet, the zealots can still live their dream, for their settlements will be legitimized in law, protected by federal authority and, in time, surrounded by Arabs who are not only fellow citizens, but also friends.

The Two Stars Plan exalts the sanctity of human life. It makes the entire Israeli-Palestinian space a safer, more secure place to be. At the same time it permits realizations of biblical prophecies that resonate with even the most conservative interpretations of scripture. Best of all, the plan achieves all of the above without sacrificing any precept of Judaic law. For nowhere in the Torah does it say Jerusalem must be under the ultimate legal sovereignty of a Jewish state (and even if it did, such a precept would be outweighed by an equivalent solution that saved lives). Insofar as American sovereignty has proven itself hospitable to a rainbow spectrum of U.S.-based Jewish sects, Jewish theologians can rest assured that the same sovereignty will be no less hospitable in the land of Judaism's birth.

Therefore, we have proven that the Two Stars Plan is not maleficent to Judaism. It protects Jewish life better than any alternative, which makes it beneficent per se. In addition, it is no less friendly to Judaism than is the United States itself, which, by general agreement, nurtures Judaism very well.

Suppose the U.S. turned hostile toward Judaism? The Israelis could revolt. If the Israelis can't suppress their Palestinian next-door neighbors, the distant Americans have scant chance of suppressing a rebellious Israeli nation.[1]

Would Americanization lead to greater Jewish assimilation? The evidence says it would not. Israel is already an increasingly Americanized society. Nevertheless, interest in Jewish religion and culture has never been higher. Avoidance of assimilation is a task for parents and local community. Government or popular culture can be made a scapegoat for assimilation, but this is illogical because it directs blame in a nonproductive direction. Popular culture has not prevented growing numbers of American Jews from celebrating their holidays and deepening their

---

1. The U.S. Constitution does not prohibit secession, although that of its seceded Confederacy did. I do not believe there is a chance in a billion that Israel would ever feel a need to secede, or that the U.S. would ever turn hostile toward such an important part of its legislative, geographic, and cultural constituency. With the confederate secession, on the other hand, Northern hostility toward slavery existed from the time of America's founding.

religious practices. While the secular nature of American society certainly *contributes* to the assimilation of many Jews, the theocratic nature of Israeli government has *not prevented* a large portion of its youth from neglecting religious obligations. The fact is that government policy and popular culture are but two of many forces that act on people, pulling them toward or away from religion. These forces are like the tides in the ocean—the trends go up and down, in and out. Great religions maintain their attractiveness to the people regardless of the superficial sparkle of popular culture.

An Israeli state in America can still be a Jewish state in the way that Utah is thought of as a Mormon state and states such as Kentucky are thought of as part of the Bible Belt. In other words, such a state will have a majority of Jews (satisfying Herzl's touchstone requirement) and will be a center of Jewish learning and culture.

Thanks to the 10th Amendment to the U.S. Constitution, vast swaths of socioeconomic authority are reserved for the states. This will enable a new Israeli-American state government to enact many laws that are Jewish-friendly, provided they fall short of showing preference to Judaism (like declaring it a state religion) or discriminating on the basis of religion. For example, an Israeli state of America could require that public (but not private) offices be closed on the Jewish Sabbath of Saturday instead of (or in addition to) the Christian Sunday Sabbath and the Muslim Friday Sabbath.[2] This would be justified because of practicality rather than a preference for Judaism. On the other hand, the state could not fund Jewish parochial schools or grant any kind of socioeconomic preferences to Jews. These constitutional limitations make Israel no less of a Jewish state—they simply ensure it is a secular Jewish state (also as preferred by Herzl) rather than a theocratic Jewish state. After surviving for thousands of years in hostile environments, Judaism does not need state support to thrive. Its intrinsic beauty enables it to thrive securely if only the state is friendly and the environment is peaceful. This is exactly what the Two Stars Plan provides.

In summary, as with Christianity and Islam, Judaism rests comfortably within the Two Stars Plan. Leaders of all three religions can bless the Two Stars Plan with a clear conscience. It serves the highest purposes of each religion. In the next chapter, we will assess whether the secular concerns of Americans, Israelis, and Palestinians are also resolved within the details of the Two Stars Plan. If so, there is a solution to the Middle-East crisis that is as practical in its details as it is elegant in its design.

---

2. Israelis already enjoy one of the shorter average workweeks amongst industrialized countries, at 37.8 hours compared to 38.5 hours in the U.S. By comparison, France has legislated a 35-hour workweek. A four-day workweek (32 hours) is likely to emerge with continued increases in productivity due to technology.

4

American Questions

The world is very different now. For man holds in his mortal hands the power to abolish all forms of human poverty and all forms of human life. And yet the same revolutionary beliefs for which our forebears fought are still at issue around the globe—the belief that the rights of man come not from the generosity of the state, but from the hand of God.

My fellow citizens of the world: ask not what America will do for you, but what together we can do for the freedom of man.

With a good conscience our only sure reward, with history the final judge of our deeds, let us go forth to lead the land we love, asking His blessing and His help, but knowing that here on earth God's work must truly be our own.

—John F. Kennedy, Inaugural Address, January 20, 1961

Americans will no doubt be intrigued by an out-of-the-box solution to Middle-East peace. However, many will immediately pounce on what they perceive to be its negatives. One can almost hear the radio talk show hosts and television talking heads moaning, "It's too far," "another Puerto Rico," "we can't afford it," "no state will give up Congressional seats for them," and "it'll worsen terrorism." Facts and logic shatter all these objections.

Distance

Israel and Palestine are 6000 miles (9500 kilometers) from Washington. Hawaii is 5000 miles (7800 kilometers) from America's capital. In other words, there is about a two-hour difference in flight time between the two.[1]

---

1. When California was admitted into the Union in 1850, it was relatively much further from the next closest state, Texas, or from the U.S. capital in Washington, than Israel is today, based on travel logistics then and now.

46

The new states would be America's first venture into the Eastern Hemisphere, but that is scarcely relevant in an age of jet travel and Internet communication.[2] Temporally, Israel and Palestine are much closer to the United States than most other states were at the time they joined the Union. Nevertheless, there will remain a "gut feeling" on the part of many Americans that the Middle East, Europe, Africa, and Asia are "beyond the reach" of American statehood. I propose that we use the neutralizing power of logic as a kind of antacid against the reflux many feel over the incorporation of distant states.

A firm tenet of U.S. foreign policy is that globalization is a good thing. A firm tenet of U.S. military policy is that force has to be deliverable to every corner of the globe. A firm tenet of U.S. social and cultural policy is that the world is like a global village. Perhaps Disney says it best: "It's a small world after all." With so much emphasis on the oneness and closeness of what Carl Sagan famously called our "pale blue dot," it is illogical to believe any place on earth is "too far" to be part of another place.

The vast continental North American distances of the 1800s were shrunk for the popular culture with the mantra of "Manifest Destiny" to stretch from "sea to shining sea." Distances that were, in fact, quite long on a pedestrian scale seemed much shorter due to ship and rail transportation, Pony Express mail, telegraph, and media familiarity. These same factors are at work today, making Middle East-North American distances seem shorter than they would be using only steamship power. It takes less than a day to travel to the Middle East, e-mail is instantaneous, telephones are ubiquitous, and both ends see each other nightly on TV. If a mantra is needed, one could say a Manifest Destiny exists for peace to stretch from the Land of Promise to the Promised Land.

The use of logic to leapfrog antiquated beliefs is what the Two Stars Plan is all about. The same U.S. Constitution that is strong enough to stretch across 200 years of time, longer than any written national constitution since the dawn of civilization, is certainly strong enough to stretch across the Atlantic and Mediterranean waters. Just as no spot on earth is too far from the long arm of the law, or from the mighty stride of human rights, it is also true that no earthly distance is too far from the reach of U.S. statehood, especially when so many other requirements have been met so admirably.

Texas or Puerto Rico?

Many Americans are likely to ask whether adding Israel and Palestine will be more like the joyful addition of the independent republic of Texas in 1845 or the

---

2. When the U.S. adopted the Monroe Doctrine in 1823, vowing to keep European nations out of the Western Hemisphere, there was no "reverse doctrine" that kept the U.S. out of the Eastern Hemisphere.

difficult romance between Puerto Rico and America. Texas was an independent country for nine years before it joined the United States.[3] Puerto Rico, on the other hand, remains a commonwealth (like a territory) of the U.S.; its people are American citizens, but a majority have never been in favor of formal American statehood. A small minority of its population would prefer to abandon its U.S. commonwealth status in favor of full, sovereign independence.

In fact, no two situations are alike. The courtship of Texas did not go smoothly (although it was all hugs at the end), and an overwhelming majority of Puerto Ricans want to retain U.S. citizenship. The decisions of Israel and Palestine to join the United States will be equally unique stories. Nevertheless, some insight can be gained by comparing the experience of a state like Texas, which people throughout the world consider emblematic of America, with that of Puerto Rico, considered by many to be a virtual colony of the U.S.

Texas became an independent republic in 1835 by breaking away from Mexico. The new Texan government immediately sought the protection of American statehood. Texans saw the same benefits of security and economic progress in statehood that would apply to Israel and Palestine. In addition, many Texans had family ties to the United States, as do many Israelis and Palestinians.[4] To the Texans' surprise, a lone U.S. Congressman (who was also a former U.S. president, John Quincy Adams) blocked a vote on the proposal and the initiative was spurned. His main objection was that Texas permitted slavery within its borders. Legislators from the powerful states of New England usually tried to limit the admission of more "slave states" into the Union.[5]

The Texans had no choice but to proceed on their own, fighting Mexico and struggling economically. Meanwhile, British agents began encouraging Texas' independence with promises of trade, seeing the state as a bulwark against American expansion westward into British Pacific Coast interests. The Mexicans, on the other hand, offered to recognize Texas' independence if it renounced any alliance with the United States. Tides changed in Washington. Concern over limiting British and Mexican influence in the Western Hemisphere vied with the ethics of slavery. The siren call of "Manifest Destiny" countered the denounce-

---

3. Vermont was also an independent country prior to joining the United States in 1791.
4. Americans were lured to Texas in the 1820s with promises of free land, much as Israelis are lured to the West Bank with promises of low-cost housing and mortgages. These new Texans revolted in part over Mexico's refusal to permit slavery.
5. Northern legislators were also wary of Southern states' tendencies to oppose high tariffs, a strong central bank, and national infrastructure improvements.

ments of the abolitionists.[6] Then, six years after spurning Texas' request to join the U.S., a new American president offered statehood to Texas.

Texan and American diplomats negotiated and proudly signed a treaty of annexation. Texans forgave the Americans for their previous rejection and showed little trust in the intentions of the British and Mexican cheerleaders for their independence. Just when all seemed to be going well, the abolitionists in the U.S. Senate used their power to block ratification of the annexation treaty. Again, Texas was slapped in the face.

Supporters of Texan statehood were not deterred. After another U.S. election appeared to better their odds, a resolution was adopted in the U.S. House of Representatives inviting Texas to become a U.S. state. The welcome was not overwhelming—120 in favor versus 98 opposed. The companion vote in the Senate succeeded by a one-vote margin, 27–25; a change of one yes to a no would have lost the majority and there was no sitting vice president at the time to break the tie. Consequently, Texas became a state by the skin of its teeth.[7] The Texan people overwhelmingly voted in favor of joining the United States. They elected their first president, Sam Houston, to be their first senator in the U.S. Senate.

Israel and Palestine, like the Republic of Texas, are already sovereign entities. In such a case, it is simply a matter of proper respect for the U.S. Congress to first offer statehood. At the urging of a modern U.S. president, much like the urging provided by President James Polk over 150 years ago, the U.S. Senate and House can pass a joint resolution. Such a resolution would invite Israel and Palestine to become states of the United States, on an equal basis with all other states. This acceptance would be subject to their submission to Congress by a date certain (one or two years off) of duly-adopted draft state constitutions that are consistent with the U.S. Constitution and with certain boundary considerations. Upon receipt of the draft constitutions, along with any accompanying resolutions of the Israeli and Palestinian legislatures and results of popular referenda, the U.S. Congress could formally pass a law making Israel and Palestine U.S. states and their peoples naturalized U.S. citizens. From that point onwards, many good things are possible, as the Texan experience has shown us all.

Puerto Rico became an American territory after it was taken from Spain in the Spanish-American War of 1898. Unlike Texas, it was not populated with

---

6. It also helped that two new "free states," Iowa and Wisconsin, were approaching readiness for statehood, counter-balancing Texas and another "slave state," Florida, which was admitted the same year.

7. The actual Constitutional vote of both houses of Congress to accept Texas into the Union succeeded by a wide margin, which followed Texas' compliance with the conditions of the barely-passed resolution. There is not a constitutional obligation for either house of Congress to first invite a place like Texas to become a state, but it is a good precedent for Israel and Palestine.

American expatriates; it was linguistically and culturally isolated from mainstream American life. During the twentieth century, its legal status was upgraded to that of a commonwealth, thereby providing its people with U.S. citizenship and greater economic benefits. A statehood movement gained steam over the decades but never succeeded in attracting a strong majority of the people. The movement competed with advocates of independence, on the one hand, and with advocates of the status quo, on the other.

The proponents of independence emphasize the value of maintaining a unique Puerto Rican culture and the pride of total self-government. However, they can never attract a majority, because most people feel the economy would fall apart without American commonwealth status. Advocates of the status quo argue that it would be a mistake to assume the burdens of statehood, such as taxation, when Puerto Ricans already have all the benefits of American citizenship, such as social-service spending, and lack only non-economic benefits, such as voting and full representation in Congress. Puerto Rican believers in the status quo represent about half the population, thereby denying statehood advocates an opportunity to achieve a majority.

The Puerto Rican experience is not likely to apply to Israel and Palestine. Instead of Puerto Rico's paralyzing three choices, Israelis and Palestinians will face a stark up-or-down decision: American statehood or not. Whereas Puerto Rico currently enjoys many of the benefits of statehood without any of the economic costs, Israel and Palestine enjoy none of the benefits of U.S. statehood and yet they incur very high economic costs via taxation and chronic insecurity. While Puerto Rico is burdened by the inertia that comes from centuries of history as a backwater in the Spanish empire, Israel and Palestine are characterized by the dynamism that comes from being front-and-center in world affairs.

It is true that Israel and Palestine do share some of the linguistic and cultural uniqueness that typifies Puerto Rico more than Texas. However, this uniqueness is not an impediment to American statehood. The pro-independence party in Puerto Rico, for whom preservation of cultural uniqueness is the paramount issue, garners no more than about 10% of the Puerto Rican vote. The pivotal issue in Puerto Rico is economics, not cultural uniqueness.

As for Israel, there is no doubt but that its cultural uniqueness can be preserved as an American state. Such uniqueness blossoms today within many American states. For example, there are Hasidic Jewish communities in Brooklyn, Miami, Los Angeles, and other urban centers. It is natural for there to be some angst, at least initially, over the loss of government funding and promotion of distinctively Jewish-Israeli culture. Let those who bemoan the loss of government involvement instead cherish the freedom that comes with independence from bureaucratic control. Under American statehood, incomes will rise and taxes will fall—these two trends auger well for increased private donations as a surefire solution to the budget gap caused by the withdrawal of government support for Judaism or other religions.

The vibrant doctrine of "states rights" within America, which gives each state plenary authority over education and cultural matters (subject only to reasonable constitutional boundaries), should also provide plenty of comfort to Palestinian advocates for cultural integrity. The U.S. Constitution is quite comfortable with Arabic being used as the primary language within Palestine (just as it is in some neighborhoods in the United States). The U.S. Constitution is also entirely conducive to Palestinian customs and traditions being widely practiced. All that is asked is for the customs and traditions to be celebrated using private rather than government resources, and that there be no discrimination against non-Palestinians and assimilated Palestinians.

Finally, just as the law clearly prohibits any U.S. state or the federal government from imposing a particular religion on the populace, it is not allergic to multiculturalism. In other words, provided that all significant groups in the population are represented, even state governments can sponsor events that highlight unique religious or cultural customs. A state-sponsored program on the wearing of the *kafiyya* is permissible so long as it also includes discussion of the *yarmulke* and secular headwear.

The main cultural concept in America is to create a large enough "tent" to accommodate a great variety of religious and ethnic customs, but not so large a tent as would collapse under permitted practices that are offensive to the sensibilities of almost everyone. America does this so well that very few Puerto Ricans fear U.S. statehood for cultural reasons. American respect for cultural integrity can be seen in states such as Texas that boast a vibrant Latino culture side-by-side with its Anglo culture. We anticipate that Israel and Palestine, as American states, will cherish each other's cultures, and general American culture, even as they nurture their own traditions, practices, and beliefs. The American tent that was big enough for Texas in 1846 is big enough for Israel and Palestine today.

Cost

The easiest voice to raise against American statehood is that "it costs too much." Such arguments arise from a mindset that "knows the price of everything and the value of nothing." The United States has, in recent years, plunked down $100 billion to militarily remove an Iraqi regime without batting an economic eye. Clearly, that decision was based on value rather than cost. The value of a permanent peace in the Middle East is so great in terms of its benefits to world stability that even an unprecedented price tag would be worth it.

Worldwide GNP today is on the order of $30 trillion. Major adverse events, such as a war involving the United States, can wipe out all or part of the 2%–4%

annual growth rate in GNP. Avoiding such a conflagration is worth that percent of the world economy, or about $600–$1200 billion. The U.S. represents about one-third of the world economy, and can thus suffer $200–$400 billion in economic costs from major world instability.

Earlier in this book an estimate was made of the costs to the U.S. budget of integrating Israel and Palestine. The principal costs accounted for were health care and social services. A net cost estimate of only $9 billion was initially arrived at, and it will be less each subsequent year as Israeli and Palestinian contributions to the U.S. economy offset their social-welfare costs. In terms of the federal budget, integrating Israel and Palestine would cause less than half a percent increase in the federal budget—much less than the impact of U.S. involvement in any Middle-East war. By comparison, the U.S. spent over $100 billion on the Marshall Plan (at today's value).

It is clear, from several different vantage points, that the U.S. can afford to absorb the multi-billion dollar costs associated with the annexation of Israel and Palestine. It is also wise to absorb those costs, because the value obtained is incalculably higher still. That value includes:

- Avoided economic losses associated with global instability induced by Middle-East crises;

- Avoided expenditures associated with a Middle-East war that almost inevitably will involve the U.S.;

- The economic contributions of the very high-tech Israeli economy and of the highly industrious Palestinian workforce;

- The moral "high ground" of including the Holy Land as part of the United States, vaguely similar to the prestige of hosting the United Nations in New York; and

- The geopolitical significance of having U.S. infrastructure securely ensconced at the crossroads of the world.

Advocates of the Two Stars Plan must be prepared for economic analyses that opponents will use as fodder for their objections. Challenge the assumptions of those economic assessments. Remember the computer axiom, garbage in, garbage out. It applies very well to the assumptions and results of computer models that underlie much economic analysis. Ask the tough questions, such as, what value will be assigned to growth in U.S., Israeli and Palestinian productivity as a result of having a frictionless economy amongst the three peoples? What value will be assigned to the hundreds or thousands of lives saved due to the avoidance of civil unrest and probable warfare? What value will be assigned to the enhanced stature of American business and diplomacy as a result of a successful incorporation of the Holy Land?

The U.S. must greatly value stability in the Middle East, because it already gives Israel over $3 billion in aid annually (which may be netted out in any cost estimates). The U.S. gives tiny Israel more foreign aid than it gives to any other country. If we value a place enough to *spend* billions of dollars a year on it without any ownership, then certainly we value it enough to *invest* billions of dollars a year in return for ownership. It is as if the U.S. is renting an apartment and now has the opportunity to purchase a condo. Assuming the place passes inspection, what wise investor would not choose to buy their flat, and thus build-up equity, rather than to continue renting only for someone else's economic benefit?

Capitol Hill

A potential showstopper for the Two Stars Plan involves the political impact within the U.S. Congress of adding two more states, and about 9 million more people. Under the U.S. Constitution, each state is allocated two senators and a number of representatives proportional to its percentage of the U.S. population, but not less than one representative. This means the current 100-person U.S. Senate would grow to 104, with an undetermined impact upon the split between Democratic and Republican Party loyalists.

More problematic is that with 9 million people, Israel and Palestine would be entitled to about twelve representatives between them. In 1929, Congress voted to limit the size of its House of Representatives to 435. Consequently, adding twelve representatives of newly-created Israeli and Palestinian congressional districts would require stripping twelve representatives from existing congressional districts. Precisely which states lost how many representatives would depend upon some simple arithmetic.[8] Clearly, the twelve states that figure to lose a Congressional seat will not be pleased.

---

8. For example, dividing America's 2000 census population of more than 280 million people by 435 representatives yields a ratio of about 646,000 citizens per representative. Hence, a state such as Montana, with 900,000 people, is entitled to one representative, whereas a state such as Idaho, with 1.3 million people, is just barely entitled to two. If the U.S. population grows by 9 million by virtue of the Two Stars Plan, it will be necessary to divide a number such as 290 million by 435 representatives, yielding a ratio of approximately 667,000 citizens per representative. As a result, Idaho would drop from two to one representatives, a fact that might well lead the Idaho Congressional delegation to oppose the Two Stars Plan.

A further political problem involves how the twelve states that stand to lose a representative will redraw their congressional districts. Each political party will attempt to use the new geographical obligation to create districts more likely to yield a majority vote for either Republicans or Democrats, based on past trends. This issue arises after each decennial census. Incorporation of Israel and Palestine could cause it to occur between censuses and could engender some opposition to the Two Stars Plan. For example, Idaho might be upset to have to lose half its Congressional delegation (from two to one representative) so that Israel can have eight and Palestine four members of the House of Representatives (assuming they are 6 million and 3 million in population, respectively). California, on the other hand, with fifty-three members in the House of Representatives, would probably not be greatly concerned over shedding one representative to accommodate the needs of two new states.

An elegant solution to avoiding Congressional hostility at the time of admitting Israel and Palestine into the United States is for Congress to add to its annexation law a provision that increases the size of the House of Representatives by twelve seats. No change has been made in the size of the House of Representatives since 1929, but the U.S. population has more than doubled since then (from 129 million to 280 million). A modest increase in the House of Representatives by the number of seats needed to accommodate Israel and Palestine before the next census seems reasonable.[9] If there is a desire to have a round number of seats in the House of Representatives, the law admitting Israel and Palestine could also increase the size of the House from 435 to 447 immediately so that the two new states have twelve seats available for election, with reapportionment to occur after the next decennial census, at which time the size of the House will be set at 450.

War against Terrorism—Don't They Hate Us?

A Pew Global Attitudes survey conducted during May 2003 revealed that a mere 1% of Jordanians and Palestinians had a favorable view of the United States. Yet

---

9. Although article 1, section 2 and 3 of the U.S. Constitution require Congressional Representatives and Senators to have been U.S. citizens for seven and nine years respectively, this is inapplicable in the context of newly-admitted states, because such states are admitted on an equal basis as the original thirteen states of America. However, there are minimum age requirements of twenty-five and thirty years, respectively. The new Israeli and Palestinian state legislatures will need to define Congressional districts of roughly equal population and hold elections. The 17th Amendment to the U.S. Constitution authorizes the governors of Israel and Palestine to appoint two U.S. senators each, pending state-wide elections for those positions.

such polls can change direction dramatically—Indonesia swung from 60% positive to 15% positive in the few months leading up to the War on Iraq. Should Americans be dissuaded by the televised images of Palestinians embracing posters of Osama bin Laden? Or, instead, should Americans realize that public opinion is like an olive tree in a strong breeze—bending one way or another, sometimes fluttering all about, but nevertheless rooted in core values, just like an apple tree?

America's founding fathers realized that public opinion is too fickle a basis for policymaking. Here are some of the steps they took to ensure that dramatic swings in early American public opinion didn't influence U.S. policy:

- Two houses of Congress had to agree on legislation, only one of which was elected proportionally to population (the House of Representatives) with the other based simply on statehood (the Senate);

- Only one-third of the Senate was elected every two years, thereby requiring two successive elections, over a period of four years, to obtain a majority of the Senate;

- The President was not elected directly by the people, but instead by "electors" chosen by each state in a number proportional to the size of their Congressional delegations;[10] and

- A unique third branch of government, the Judiciary, had the power to invalidate legislation deemed inconsistent with the Constitution,[11] thereby necessitating a very protracted Constitutional amendment process, should the public insist upon such radical legislation. The judges that comprise this branch are appointed for life, making them largely immune to the vicissitudes of public opinion.

---

10. There are currently 538 presidential electors, one for each seat in the House and the Senate, plus three for the District of Columbia. This system gives less populous states an influence in presidential elections that is larger than what it would be with direct popular voting because every state gets two seats in the Senate and one seat in the House, regardless of population. Israel and Palestine would each be entitled to about ten and six presidential electors respectively, giving each state presidential election influence comparable to Georgia and Connecticut.
11. This power, known as "judicial review," is only implicitly stated in the Constitution, but has been well-accepted for over 200 years, after its establishment in the famous case of *Marbury vs. Madison*.

In essence, the Founding Fathers required three separate branches of government, one of which consisted of two sub-branches (House and Senate), to agree on legislation. Each branch was kept at arm's length from direct public opinion. This structure reveals the profound realization among some very wise men that public opinion should not be taken too seriously. The shape of a tree under a strong breeze is not its true shape.

Americans can, therefore, follow the lead of their founding fathers and not be influenced by the results of overseas opinion polls or boisterous demonstrations for the benefit of television news crews. Anyone who has actually been to Palestine, Israel, or even places like Iraq and Iran, will, I trust, agree with the following statement: common people everywhere, and especially in the Middle East, like Americans very much. The opposition to America that they express is opposition to American government policies, not to the American people. One cannot walk more than a few steps through the alleyways of the Arab Quarter of old Jerusalem, or the Sepah district of Tehran, without bumping into a local who asks if you know his brother, uncle, or cousin in Texas, Iowa, or North Carolina.

If Palestinians or Israelis do not want to be part of America, they will vote not to accept an invitation to join. If they do vote to join, then they must not hate Americans. No one makes an enemy the commander-in-chief of their military units or accepts an enemy's constitution as the ultimate law of their land. I am confident that Israelis and Palestinians feel a great sense of kinship with the American people. They will accept an American invitation to join the union because they know they share common values with the American people. They also know that merging military forces and statutory laws is their best hope for peace, security, and a good quality of life.

A conspiracy theorist might hypothesize that union with the United States will be accepted as a ruse to promote terrorism. One can almost hear the radio "shock jock" explaining how Israel and Palestine are little more than al-Quaeda Trojan Horses, unloading busloads of suicide bombers once American statehood brings them safely within the passport control borders of the United States. In general, statehood opponents may ask, how can the U.S. fight terrorism if it brings a hotbed of terrorism within its national borders? How can the U.S. succeed in wiping out terrorists if it makes thousands of terrorists or potential terrorists constitutionally-protected American citizens?

The answer to all of the terrorist-related concerns is that the Two Stars Plan does nothing to increase the flow of terrorists into the United States. America already has some of the most porous national borders in the world. All one needs to enter the country legally is a round-trip air ticket, a little bit of money, and a passport that comes up clean in a five-second computerized scan at an airport. Can anyone doubt that a terrorist network supplies these three things?

Furthermore, one could fill a shelf with three-inch binders describing in detail all of the different ways to enter the United States illegally. Certainly the tons of marijuana, hashish, cocaine, and heroine flooding American streets are not declared at customs! It defies reality to claim that American statehood would increase the flow of terrorists past the Statue of Liberty's welcoming arm.

This point the conspiracy theorists may concede but they might then ask: why add thousands of potential terrorists to the U.S. population via American statehood? Why not at least make them sweat a bit to sneak into the country? The answer to these queries involves one part caution against stereotyping, one part respect for the role of homeland defense, and one part realization that there are no risk-free solutions to major problems.

It is no fairer to paint Israelis and Palestinians as potential terrorists than it is to paint African-Americans as potential rapists, Asians as potential spies, or Mississippians as potential racists. It *may* be true that, compared to some background population, a higher percentage of people from the Middle East are terrorists, just as a higher percentage of people from Italy are good cooks. But reliance upon this factoid will lead one to error the great majority of the time. Consider the following example. Suppose 5% of Mississippians are racists, compared to 2% of all Americans. Suppose further that a person who doesn't like racists receives a great job offer in Jackson, Mississippi. Even though 95% of their encounters with people will be free of racism, they will lose out on a great opportunity if they rely on the factoid.

In fact, there is no data at all to indicate that people from the Middle East are more or less prone to suicidal terrorism than Americans. Waco and Jonestown are just two of many names that are associated with American suicidal fanaticism. Oklahoma City was the result of purebred American terrorism. There are more guns in America than people, and more underground militantly anti-Government groups than the FBI has field offices. Others tend to think of Middle-Eastern people as being prone to terrorism because their faces are frequently flashed across the television screen as examples. But it has to be recalled that the region is in the midst of a de facto civil war and much of the population is under military control. How many American acts of terrorism would there be in similar circumstances?[12]

---

12. The British loathed Jewish terrorism prior to Israel's independence, and it is said to have turned Churchill against Zionism. England abstained on the UN vote of Israeli statehood under the 1947 Partition Plan. One of the saddest incidents involved the assassination in 1948 of Swedish Count Folke Bernadotte, a UN mediator in Jerusalem who had been instrumental in saving about 21,000 Jews from the Nazis during World War II.

There is data that shows that the vast majority of Israelis and Palestinians are calm, peace-loving people. Their rates of common violent crime are below those in the United States. Only a miniscule percentage of their peoples have ever been involved in a terrorist act. Stereotyping always leads to error, so it is important that it not be allowed to infect our decision-making on such a vital matter as the Two Stars Plan.

It should also be recalled that, even if additional terrorists do slip into the U.S. as a result of the Two Stars Plan, we have an increasingly effective Homeland Defense system to guard against any harm they might do. Homeland Defense operates on the same "universal precaution" theory as does the practice of modern medicine—one must assume that all bodily fluids may be infectious just as one must assume that all people may be terrorists. One cannot afford to assume terrorists look, speak, or act in any particular way, just as one cannot afford to think someone who is HIV+ looks, acts, or speaks a certain way. Consequently, the types of homeland-security measures that are being taken are the same whether or not Israel and Palestine become American states. A country must be able to give itself a maximum level of protection against terrorism consistent with its tolerance for socio-economic hassles and civil-rights compromises. Given that a country such as the U.S. is operating under this regime, it changes nothing to add the United States two new states that have experienced a heightened level of terrorism in the past.

The last part of the response to terrorist-based hand-wringing over the Two Stars Plan is that for every benefit there is a cost. It has been shown above that terrorists do not need statehood in order to infiltrate the U.S., that stereotyping Middle Eastern people as terrorists is logically wrong and morally unfair, and that homeland defense must necessarily already assume a greater level of terrorist risk than is currently experienced. Despite these factors, assuming *in arguendo* that statehood did give rise to a heightened period of terrorism, the Two Stars Plan is still the right thing to do.

An ultimate purpose of the Two Stars Plan is to help win the war on terrorism by eliminating the Middle East crisis as a principal source of fuel for terrorism's flames. Many medicines make patients feel worse before they feel better. This is called a detoxification reaction. In a similar vein, the Two Stars Plan is a systematic solution to a centuries-old problem. Some detoxification reaction may indeed occur. But, with Homeland Defense, we have the necessary tools in place to contain any such reaction. The certain benefit of a just and lasting peace in the Holy Land easily outweighs the possibility of a brief and well-contained cost.

In sum, Americans are the ultimate pragmatists and are likely to view the Two Stars Plan in that light. Are these states too far? Heck no, it takes only two hours longer to fly from Washington to its newest states' capital, Jerusalem, than to its most recent state's capital, Honolulu. Is it going to cost too much or cause taxes to go up? Negative. First year net costs should not exceed $9 billion, about 0.5% of the federal budget and only a tenth the cost of one year in Iraq. Some cost estimates will come in higher, and some will come in lower. The real point is that the value of the Two Stars Plan is incalculably high because of its unique contribution to world peace and to America's culture.

Politics is the art of the pragmatic, so here, too, Americans will consider the Congressional headcount implications of the Two Stars Plan. Will it disadvantage either Republicans or Democrats? Will it favor small states or large states? In fact, the Two Stars Plan should be neutral with regard to all of these considerations. Especially if implemented as proposed, with a long-overdue modest increase in the size of the House of Representatives, the addition of Israeli and Palestinian congressmen will have no material impact on Capitol Hill.

Finally, Americans will ask themselves, "What are we getting into? Do these people even like us? Will we regret our actions?" As described above, Israelis and Palestinians do like Americans. Most have American relatives or good friends. While they can get angry at U.S. government policies, that makes them even more like ordinary Americans. And while they do have their extremists, how many times have we heard that some federal court permitted yet another U.S. flag burning? The fact is that Israeli and Palestinian extremists are few in number and are drawn out of the woodwork by the problems that the Two Stars Plan resolves.

The situation is analogous to the admission into the United States of the independent Republic of Texas. Proud Texans weren't going to beg for admission, but once properly invited, they voted overwhelmingly to join. While there were costs in terms of dollars and lives associated with the incorporation of Texas, no sane person today would doubt that it was in the best interests of both Texans and Americans to hook up. The same is true of Israelis, Palestinians, and Americans today.

5

Israeli Issues

Israel wants to be a Jewish state, a democratic state, and a big state, safe in its boundaries. But it can choose only two of these goals, because another people lives in this land. We can be great and democratic, but we will not be able to build a solely Jewish state. We can be Jewish and democratic, but then we shall have to give up a part of the territory. We can be a big Jewish nation, but not democratic, because we will have to limit the rights of the Palestinians who live alongside us.

—David Ben-Gurion, 1948

For the thoughtful Israeli, the Two Stars Plan creates an unnerving tension between the heart and the mind. The mind swiftly weighs the pros and cons, calculating with ease a large balance in favor of U.S. statehood. The heart hesitates, coughs with unease, and gazes longingly at the wistful dream of a big, democratic Jewish country. Israel has come a huge distance in half a century of independence. She has achieved most of her goals, which is a great deal more than most countries can say. Who can easily say goodbye to a nurturing home? All the logic in the world only softens the blows life imposes upon the gentle heart.

The purpose of this chapter is to soften the impact upon the Israeli heart of merging with the United States. Israelis may well feel that they have the most to lose. For Americans, the merger is something relatively small in the grand scheme of things. After all, Israel and Palestine's ten million people would represent only 3% of the U.S. population. For Palestinians, the merger is a dramatic improvement over non-statehood, proto-statehood or military occupation. Even though the vision of an independent sovereign country will not be realized, it would be transmuted into that of a proud and unique American state. Something ephemeral is turned into something real. But, for the Israelis, something real, their nation, is being converted into something less real, a promise of equal statehood, with peace and prosperity.

The Israelis are taking the biggest risk of the three players. But Israelis also have the most to gain. Israelis have good examples of risk-taking to consider. The Jews who heeded Herzl's call and fled Europe for Israel before the rise of Nazism risked a lot, but gained much more. The Jews who fled Eastern Europe for America around 1900 risked all they knew and had, but also gained a great deal more. Two thousand years of Diaspora has bred a strong risk-taking strain into the Jewish character. This predisposition has now entered its ideal environmental challenge. Rise to the risk and trade the life of a big fish in a chronically threatened small pond for the life of a smaller fish in a secure large pond! Trade dead-end sovereignty for open-ended union. It is in this way, and only in this way, that healthy growth will be possible for generations.

Anti-Semitism and the Jewish Question

Foremost among most Israelis' fears will be threats to survival. Will the Jewish Question (what to do with non-conforming Jews in predominantly gentile countries), dormant since this birth of Israel, raise its ugly head once again? Will Israel be overrun with non-Jews, recreating a minority status most have never known? Has America finally overcome its own anti-Semitism? Can America be counted on to defend Israel?

Pages of evidence about the great bond between America and Israel cannot vanquish a lurking fear of abandonment.[1] Examples such as the Orthodox Jewish vice presidential candidate, Joe Lieberman, who secured half the American vote, will not quash the concerns of those world-weary Israelis who, as a matter of principle, never fully trust non-Jews and rarely trust fellow Jews. Even hard statistics, such as the disproportionately large number of Jews in the U.S. Supreme Court (12% of the Justices versus 2% of the population), in Congress (11% of the Senate, 6% of the House, and 33% of state congressional delegations), and in every kind of American citadel of excellence will fail to calm the nerves of a person who believes "only the paranoid survive."

---

1. In 1967, the U.S. spectacularly abandoned Israel by failing to live up to its 1956 guarantees of Israeli access to waterways such as the Straits of Tiran, thus precipitating the Six Day War. Earlier, in 1947, U.S. support for the UN Partition and establishment of Israel occurred only because President Truman overcame objections from his own State and Defense Departments, which was so firm the U.S. delegate in charge of the matter at the UN resigned upon Truman's recognition of Israel. Truman, on the other hand, seemed to be influenced by fear of losing votes to Republicans over the matter, as well as intense Jewish lobbying, and not by any reliably firm orientation in favor of Israeli independence.

As it is impossible to disprove a negative, it is impossible to dismiss a belief that Israelis cannot rely upon anyone but themselves for their survival. For, even though one could make a long list of Israel's friends over the past half-century, and one could enumerate the billions of dollars donated to Israel, the skeptic would still claim that all such aid arose because of the efforts of Israelis to procure the same. To these hardheaded Israelis, there is but one answer: In the unlikely event that America fails you, you can always take your country back. The Israeli Defense Force will still be there (uniform changes take but a few minutes), your personal firearms will still be in your closet, and you will still be 10,000 kilometers closer to Jerusalem than is the Pentagon. So take the chance for a greater future; nothing irretrievable will be lost.

The large majority of Israelis are not so hardheaded. They will just be nervous about leaving the shore they know, sovereign Israel, for a land they know not, an Israeli state in the United States. While anti-Semitism lurks in dark corners throughout the United States, it cannot thrive anywhere reachable by the long arm of the federal government. Prejudice and discrimination exists in Israel as well, and few Israelis expect any kind of heaven on earth to arise soon. America is not Germany before World War II. There is no Jewish Question in America. Americans hardly care whether Jews assimilate or not. America is not the France witnessed by Herzl. Junk bond king Michael Milken was no Dreyfus, for the tycoon was no more taken down because he was Jewish than was Worldcom taken down because it was full of Southern Baptists. Even a Hasidic Jew is no more unusual on American streets than a Purda-enclosed woman with *hijab* and *burqa* or a white-turbaned Sikh. This is the age of diversity, and America already is, in many key respects, a nation of minorities. In such a nation, any one minority, such as the Jews, can feel safe.

Better still for Israeli Jews, however, is that they have a double-layer of safety. First, as just noted, Jews in America are an almost invisible minority in a nation of minorities. Second, in Israel they have the comfort of being in the majority. While no people have a greater right to be paranoid about discrimination than the Jews, the Two Stars Plan provides Jews with no less protection from discrimination than they currently enjoy. In fact, it provides Jews with strategic long-term protection against discrimination by removing from the modern anti-Semite's quiver his favorite poison-tip arrow—the chronic Middle-East peace problem.

An influx of Gentiles or Arabs into a new state of Israel is also not a credible fear. People do not move very easily, and when they do it is usually for economic advantage or better overall quality of life. While more American Jews may well move to Israel once it becomes safer as an American state, it is difficult to imagine many Gentiles wanting to take such a long leap. The standard of living in Israel is lower than in most of the U.S., and the competition is fierce. On the other hand, Gentile tourism to the Holy Land will almost certainly experience a huge boom.

As to drowning in a sea of Arabs, the existence of a proud state of Palestine next door to Israel makes this scenario less likely than ever before. Israel does already count over one million Arabs among its citizens, and this population has a higher birthrate than does the Jewish demographic. Nevertheless, this population is far outnumbered by Jews. For both economic reasons (lower housing costs, hassle-free travel between the two new American states) and cultural reasons (pride of living in a Palestinian-controlled homeland, greater linguistic harmony) many among Israel's Arab population, as well as most Palestinian refugees, will choose to make their primary residence in Palestine rather than in Israel. Consequently, the Two Stars Plan makes it less likely than the status quo for Jews to end up as a minority within Israel.

Israelis whose hearts belong to God know that it is not earthly government, Israeli or American, that keeps them safe. To the Israeli who trusts only in his weapons, keep them at ready in your house.[2] To the Israeli whose heart yearns for a return to the days of fearless bus trips and market days, American statehood will make that a fact. To the Israeli whose heart beats with pride at the sight of her flag, at the accomplishments of her people, and at the daily ubiquity of her culture, American statehood gives to you a yet louder, stronger drum upon which your song of pride may be played. The American shores to which the Two Stars Plan asks Israelis to sail requires no sacrifice of security, pride, or culture. It represents yet a larger platform upon which Israeli society can continue to advance.

The Diaspora

Part of the tug between the Israeli's heart and mind over the Two Stars Plan will involve The Diaspora. Israelis are proud that they provide a safe haven to Jews anywhere in the world. Most Israelis are themselves beneficiaries of this safe haven, known as the Right of Return, either personally or via their parents or grandparents. To settle the Israeli heart, there must be a strong pledge that they may continue to provide a safe haven for Jews in Diaspora.

---

2. The Second Amendment to the U.S. Constitution, which prohibits the federal government from denying individuals the right to retain firearms, does not apply to states. This means that it is up to Israel and Palestine, as U.S. states, what kind of gun control they wish to implement. Of course, such gun control, being state action, must comply with equal protection and therefore be applied in a reasonable and non-discriminatory manner.

As described in Chapter 2, the Two Stars Plan fully resolves issues relating to the Diaspora. Foreign Jews (and non-Jews) could apply for a "Right of Return" visa under a new special category of people willing to settle in Israel. The number of such visas could be set at the current average number of immigrants to Israel, about 70,000 per year. In fact, the majority of people immigrating to Israel today are not Jewish under religious law. These mostly Russian immigrants simply claim Jewish ancestry in order to take advantage of the Right of Return law. Their goal is to garner a better life as compared to opportunities in former Soviet Republics.

The best news for Israelis concerned with obligations to the Diaspora is that the Two Stars Plan reunites six million Jews in Israel with a like number of Jews in America. In essence, the Two Stars Plan ends the wandering for the largest number of Jews in Diaspora, the American Jews. Aside from this intellectual point, the much greater safety of an American-Israeli state will energize tens of thousands of American Jews to move to Israel. These intellectual and practical points should certainly calm the Israeli heart.

Politics

It is sometimes joked that for every two Israelis there are three political opinions. Those opinions are voiced vigorously in cafes as well as in the Knesset. Israelis must love their politics because they have so many political parties. What will happen to Israeli politics under the American two-party system? Can Israelis be comforted that their Knesset will continue to function as a fertile breeding ground for shifting alliances among a kaleidoscope of political parties?

Nothing in the Two Stars Plan requires Israel to change its basic political system. The U.S. Constitution does not require American states to have any particular legislative system, provided they have a government that complies with the general principles of a democracy. So, even though only one of America's current fifty states, Nebraska, has a unicameral legislature, there is no problem with Israel maintaining its unicameral legislature, the Knesset. Indeed, several American states are considering shifting to a unicameral legislature due to the purported greater cost-effectiveness of that approach. Similarly, even though all American states elect their legislators on a district-based, winner-take-all principle (the top vote-getter in a geographically-defined area becomes the sole legislative representative of that area), there is no problem with Israel continuing to elect its Knesset members with a state-wide proportional voting system (political parties get to seat legislators in proportion to the percentage of the total vote the party receives, subject to a 1.5% limit). Hence, if Israel has nineteen political parties in the Knesset today, it may have as many in its Knesset even when the Knesset becomes the state legislature.

A separate issue involves the voting for Israel's Senators and Representatives, as part of America's national elections. In all existing American states, Congressional candidates run against each other within a particular district. The vote-winner in that district becomes the sole representative. The U.S. Constitution does not insist on this method, and in the 1800s, some states enjoyed multi-member districts that were amenable to proportional voting, as in Israel. However, article 1, section 4 of the Constitution does give Congress the right to set nationwide rules, and Congress has mandated single-member districts since 1967.

Thus, the Israelis could not currently deem their entire state to be one congressional district and elect as their representatives the individuals supported by political parties in proportion to the percentage of the state-wide vote that such parties received. For example, based on population, Israel should be entitled to have about eight U.S. representatives. The mandated American method would require that Israel's Knesset divide Israel into eight distinct geographical districts of roughly equal population. Then, the largest vote-getter in each district would be its sole representative in the U.S. Congress.

A more Israeli-flavored approach, which is not currently permitted for an American state, is for the Knesset to consider all of Israel as one congressional district to be represented by eight representatives. The eight representatives would be allocated to political parties in proportion to the percentage of the state-wide vote that such political parties received. A political party that has 20% support nationwide, and no more than 20% support in any geographical area, would get no U.S. Congressional representation with the current American approach, but it would get at least one U.S. Representative in the Israeli-flavored approach. Nevertheless, Israelis may continue to use proportional voting for their state legislature, the Knesset. The winner-take-all, single-member district approach for Congressional elections will provide Israelis with some good experience in a less factional approach to politics.

The Israeli proportional voting system may, however, be used in selecting Israel's U.S. presidential electors. For example, the Israeli Knesset may decide that its ten or so presidential electors will be allocated to party representatives in accordance with that party's percentage of the popular vote. A disadvantage of this approach is that it would tend to dilute Israel's overall impact in a U.S. presidential election, because it would likely be able to offer any one candidate only a fraction of its allocated number of electors. Indeed, it is for this reason that most U.S. states have adopted winner-take-all approaches to presidential elections. With more electors available than states such as Connecticut, Georgia, and Virginia, Israel could be sure to attract keen attention from U.S. presidential candidates.

Economics

Every new solution should be test-driven past the German word *Schlimmbesserung,* which means an improvement that actually makes things worse. "HOV (high-occupancy-vehicle) lanes" reserved for carpoolers on busy highways in an effort to reduce congestion are a great example of *Schlimmbesserung.* Instead, congestion worsens in direct proportion to the one of three, four, or five lanes taken out of general use. The HOV lane taunts everyone with its emptiness.

Previous chapters have shown that *Schlimmbesserung* does not apply to the Two Stars Plan in the realms of security, politics, social services, health care, and cultural integrity. In all of these areas, the Two Stars Plan affects either an unambiguous improvement over the status quo (e.g., security) or imposes no detriment (e.g., politics). The purpose of this section is to assess whether the average Israeli will be better off, worse off, or unaffected economically after union with the United States. Provided they are not worse off, the risk of *Schlimmbesserung* can be definitively crossed off the geopolitical checklist of what to avoid.

As of 2003, Israel's per capita GDP stood at $17,710, about 57% of U.S. levels, whereas Israel's cost of living was 93% that of New York City. Clearly, this means Israelis are, in general, struggling economically compared to Americans. They make about half as much money as Americans, but have to pay out almost the same costs. Generally speaking, and subject to a closer review of specifics below, merger will have the effect of raising Israeli income levels, bringing them on par with the rest of the United States. This will significantly improve the economic lives of ordinary Israelis.

There are many reasons for the current economic discrepancy between Israel and the United States. She has absorbed many more people, as a percentage of her population, than has the U.S. in recent years. At the same time, warfare, geographical isolation, and substantial government bureaucracy limit growth in her GDP. The *Economist* magazine ranks Israel's business environment as the 24th best in the world, which is quite good but still a long way off from the number-two ranking accorded the United States. Living costs remain high due to the security-conscious infrastructure (9% of GDP is spent on defense compared to 3% in the U.S.), high level of taxation (petroleum costs are among the highest in the world), and large number of American dollars driving up the cost of Israeli goods and services (America is Israel's largest trading partner). Italy makes for an interesting comparison. Israel's per-capita income is about the same as Italy's, but it is much more expensive to live everyday in Israel than in Italy.

As part of the United States, Israeli salaries and employment levels can be expected to quickly be on par with those of the U.S. From an infrastructure standpoint, Israel has everything a high-tech company would want—except that it is a chronic war zone as opposed to a peaceful part of the United States. Israel is in the top five countries in the world in terms of R&D spending as a percent of GDP, top ten countries in the world in terms of education spending, and top twenty countries in terms of the percent of the population in college. She is ranked by experts as tied with the U.S. for being the sixteenth least corrupt country out of 200 candidates, better than Germany and Japan. She has the telephone-line density of economic powerhouses such as Korea and Singapore, and has the world's seventh highest mobile-phone density (surpassing even Sweden and Finland). America has never absorbed a place as advanced as Israel. In many respects, Israel is more developed than the U.S.

Israel does not *need* merger with the United States for economic reasons. Even if Israelis have to squeeze their shekels more than Americans have to stretch their dollars, the Israeli quality of life is good. Israeli life expectancy is sixth highest in the world (America comes in at number twenty-eight), divorce rates are less than half of America's, and its Human Development Index ranking of twenty-second in the world is consistent with other Southern EU countries (the U.S. ranks number six; Norway currently holds the top spot). The main point is that merger with the U.S. is very unlikely to degrade the Israeli economy. In all likelihood, as part of the U.S., Israeli unemployment will fall and salaries will rise. Israeli exports will cease being stigmatized by the Middle-East crisis and will start benefiting from the positive imprimatur, "Made in the USA."

Schlimmbesserung may now be crossed off the checklist. Merger with the U.S. is no HOV lane. It is, instead, more like the cloverleaf that joins one highway with another. Everyone benefits by being able to travel farther and faster. Surely there are times when people pine for more pastoral days. Fortunately, there are always kibbutzim, communes, and national parks that offer non-automotive experiences. But very few among us would give up the car, the highway, or the interchange. And no Israeli should oppose the Two Stars Plan out of fear that there may be some hidden economic costs. There won't be; all of the net economic benefits will flow to Israel. As mentioned above, Israel has the most to gain.

Culture

Even with confidence that American statehood makes them more secure, and with assurance that they will be no worse off economically, Israeli hearts may still tartle over the prospect of unleashing overwhelming Americanization on their delightfully ethnic land. To this fear there is a crystal clear answer: cultural homogenization does *not* have to be swallowed along with the Two Stars Plan.

In the American system, states and localities have the authority, through the use of zoning laws, to control the look and feel of their communities. States such as Vermont have used this power to eliminate billboards from her highways. Towns such as Columbia, Maryland, have used this power to prohibit gauche or crassly commercial storefronts. Cities can even extend their cultural reach into the fifth estate by approving cable-television companies, newsstand locations, and building permits for movie theatres.

There are some constitutional limits to the exercise of local zoning authority. The cultural controls must be adopted with due process and in a non-arbitrary manner. They must be implemented fairly, without singling out particular companies, products, or information content for discriminatory action. For example, an Israeli town could not permit only kosher hamburger stands, but it could restrict all hamburger stands to specific locations and limit the size of their signs.

"Americanization" means different things to different people. To some, it may mean strip malls littered with immigrant start-up retail businesses, while to others it may mean a certain homogenization of storefronts as a slate of 100 or so franchise names blanket the commercial landscape. For some, it may mean the subjugation of ancestral culture to a popular culture centered about shopping, television series, and cars. But to others it may mean a smorgasbord of ancestral cultures that are nurtured in countless homes, restaurants, and places of worship. In this latter view, the shallow popular culture is just background static, like the din of traffic in a big city. Just what is it about "Americanization" that many Israelis will be worried about? Is not Israel itself full of strip malls, storefront chains, shallow popular culture, and a smorgasbord of ancestral cultures?

Israel's strip malls, storefront chains, and popular culture all have a Hebraic flavor to them. Even if the structure is American, the content is Jewish. The hamburger stand may say McDonald's, but the menu is in Hebrew, falafel is offered, and on Passover there is a substitute for leavened buns. The Americanization that many Israelis feel tepid about is the un-Jewish content, not the business-efficient structure. Fortunately, this is a problem that free enterprise can resolve.

Businesses that don't cater to Israeli tastes and sensitivities will not succeed. Marketplace forces will ensure that Israelis get the flavor of Americanization that they want. Indeed, it is these same market forces that make San Antonio look so different from Boston. America's southwestern culture is quite different from its northeastern culture, and businesses are smart enough to put the right culture in the right place. Savvy Israeli entrepreneurs have been doing this well for years. The Two Stars Plan will bring more tourists, and it will bring more income to most Israelis. But nothing in the Two Stars Plan subjugates a culture such as Israel's that is loved in its surroundings. To do so would be unprofitable, and that is most assuredly un-American!

It is only natural for Israeli hearts to pause at the prospect of merging with America. On careful consideration, though, the heart may follow the mind with calm assurance. Union risks neither physical nor economic survival and impinges upon neither local politics nor national culture. The Two Stars Plan addresses emotional reasons to hesitate as well as it does logical reasons to proceed. Union with America is the next step in the cultural evolution of the Israeli people. It lets Israel be a vibrant part of a great nation, a progressive arm of a democratic union, and a safe haven for the entire spectrum of Jewish faith. By using a global rather than a regional measuring stick, it is possible to hit all three of Israel's aspirations: greatness, democracy, and Judaism. For such a grand achievement, it is worth it to rise to the challenge and to take the measured risk.

6

Palestinian Perspectives

Israelis must abandon the myth that it is possible to have peace and occu-pation at the same time, that peaceful coexistence is possible between slave and master. The lack of Israeli security is born of the lack of Palestinian freedom. Israel will have security only after the end of occupation, not before…Once Israel and the rest of the world understand this funda-mental truth, the way forward becomes clear: End the occupation, allow the Palestinians to live in freedom and let the independent and equal neighbors of Israel and Palestine negotiate a peaceful future with close eco-nomic and cultural ties.

—Marwan Barghouti, *Washington Post*, 2002.

Her eyes and the tattoo on her hands are Palestinian,
Her name, Palestinian,
Her dreams and sorrow, Palestinian,
Her kerchief, her feet and body, Palestinian,
Her words and her silence, Palestinian,
Her voice, Palestinian,
Her birth and her death, Palestinian.

—Mahmoud Darwish, *The Lover.*

In physics it is said that for every action there is an equal and opposite reaction. So it is as well in matters of socio-cultural identity and nationalism, but with incalculable complexity. Just as heavy steps in fertile earth leave corresponding footprints in their wake, so do large impositions upon a settled people see a new culture rise in response. When tens of thousands of European Jews arrived in Ottoman Palestine shortly before and after 1900, it was as if a blue dye had been sprinkled upon a yellow liquid. By the law of action and reaction, of pressure and imprint, the entire solution turned green with Palestinian identity. The sudden

70

appearance of Zionists in their midst, before even the age of air travel, quickened a Palestinian national consciousness. It formed from the intersecting Arab, Christian, and Moslem identities that populated the loosely-ruled Ottoman provinces associated with Beirut, Syria, and Gaza.

A number of other factors helped to congeal a particularly steadfast Palestinian identity with remarkable speed. Local intellectuals read about peoples all over the world clamoring for independence from distant or ethnically-distinct rule. "Shouldn't this apply to Arabs in the Ottoman Empire?" they whispered to themselves in secret meetings and literary clubs. How about to Arabs living in Palestine, with their unique attachments to their ancient towns and their tight orbit about Jerusalem?

In 1876, one hundred years after the American Revolution, the Turks adopted a constitution that stipulated freedom of press and local elections to a Constantinople-based parliament. Within a decade or two, the people living in Jaffa, the Galilee, Nablus, Jerusalem, and Gaza saw themselves reflected for the first time in the mirrors of parliamentary debate and local newsprint. They saw themselves addressed as "Palestinians," and they saw clearly the existence of grievances unique to their people. They angered as a Palestinian region when the center, in Constantinople, did little to address complaints raised by their elected representatives.

Foremost of their grievances was loss of control over their ancestral lands. The problem began in the 1850s, when Ottoman land registration and property-tax laws had the effect of dispossessing peasants in what is now Israel and Palestine (but was then known as southern Syria) of hereditary lands. Vast tracts of the Holy Land thus fell under the legal ownership of wealthy absentee landlords, or under the Turkish government. This was something else to "become Palestinian" about. But this motivating factor took on namesake force when European Jews began purchasing the large tracts of land from absentee owners who cared very little for the interests of the peasants living on the land. By the time local intellectuals read reports that Herzl's followers had chosen to buy up as much of the Holy Land (instead of Herzl's other choice, remote Argentina) as the home for the *Judenstaat*, it was time to either "be Palestinian or be gone." The Palestinian nation was sharply defined further by the culture clash between rapidly-increasing numbers of European Jews on messianic missions and the static population of local, largely-agrarian Arabic peasants, with their deeply-rooted, merchant-class Christian Arab brethren.

The Israelis helped forge a Palestinian national identity by giving indigenous peoples a survival-based cause behind which to unite. In much the same way, over a century earlier, the British helped forge an American national identity by giving struggling colonists a set of noble causes to champion. This is how national identity forms: action/reaction, footstep/footprint, blue + yellow = green. Israel itself must thank the Palestinians for their reciprocal role in shaping its national character, just as the ancient Greeks absorbed stoicism and other traits from their conquered lands to the East.

Israeli culture is no older than Palestinian culture, nor does either's national consciousness predate the other. Israeli culture is not the same as Jewish culture, just like Palestinian culture is not identical to Arabic or Islamic culture. Modern cultures are not equivalent to their ancient inspirations. Both Israel and Palestine can trace the important memes that contribute to their cultures back across the centuries and even millennia. But each nation's first stirrings are scarcely one hundred years old, and each symbiotically grew in reaction to its twin. Israel has been more successful in establishing her national identity, but she also had vastly more international assistance than did the Palestinians.[1] Israel's ancient inspiration was also more concrete, reflected as a Kingdom in the Torah, Bible, and Koran. However, this fact in no way diminishes the credibility of Palestinian culture. None of us wish to be ruled by archaeologists or their discoveries.

Our key question is whether these or other unique aspects of the Palestinian experience alter the feasibility of the Two Stars Plan. Is it really necessary for Palestine to squander years as a struggling standalone country before it reaps the benefits of merger with the U.S.? Or can Palestine be like the smart developing country that bypasses investment in an archaic wired telephone network and goes straight to universal wireless service? In other words, are the Palestinian people able to leapfrog over post-colonial nationhood and advance straight to an equal membership in a twenty-first century union?

This chapter will explore these questions by assessing the ability of the Two Stars Plan to handle issues that are sensitive to Palestinians. These are the emotion-stirring issues that Palestinians have long hoped their nation-state would address. If these issues can be resolved as well, or better, by making Palestinian a state in the United States, then the Two Stars Plan fares well. For it will be able to both resolve uniquely Palestinian concerns as well as provide superior outcomes on matters of importance to people everywhere: safety, security, economic opportunity, and good quality of life.

---

1. Israel's high moral ground was that foreign patrons linked the new Israeli nationalists (i.e., the Zionists) to the ancient Jews, but only linked the new Palestinian nationalists (i.e., the indigenous people) to the defeated Ottomans. In fact, both sets of nationalist aspirations were new (hence, Herzl's efforts to *persuade* Jews to adopt his *Judenstaat* goal), even though both peoples had ancient roots in the land. As Native Americans know all too well, ancient roots don't count for much legally, although at times they can help win sympathy.

National Aspirations and the Palestinian Question

It is ironic that just when the Palestinians are getting their own nation-state, those post-feudal creations are going out of fashion. Newly-liberated former Soviet satellites in Eastern Europe are falling over each other to cede sovereignty to the transnational European Union. It is a bit soon to declare single-state nations moribund, but multi-state unions are the wave of the future. Old-fashioned money-printing and passport-issuing nation-states will become backwaters.

Just as backwater beats no water, an old-fashioned country-state sounds good if it is the only alternative to statelessness. However, these are not the only options available to the Palestinian people. Their national aspirations can be abundantly satisfied as a Palestinian-majority state, on the West Bank and Gaza, in the United States. The Palestinian Question can be definitively answered as follows:

- The Palestinians are a people, with their own history and culture, and their right to preserve and honor that nationality will be protected under the U.S. Constitution, giving them the same opportunities as every other culture that thrives in the U.S.

- The Palestinians have a homeland, which consists of that part of Israeli-Palestinian space that was not allocated to Israel under the 1949 Armistice, specifically Gaza, the West Bank, and East Jerusalem. This homeland will be forever protected from occupation as an equal state, named Palestine, in the United States of America.

- The Palestinians have a future. As Americans, Palestinians will have freedom to travel, study, and live in any American state, and they will have access to the abundant economic opportunities of the world's largest capital and job market.

These answers to the Palestinian question trump those from any other paradigm. With these answers the Palestinian is first an American, but is no less a Palestinian who may or may not (as he chooses) live in the state of Palestine. With these answers, the Palestinian is assured of his or her civil rights, including the freedom to transfer their heritage to their children in secular public or religious private schools, and the freedom to criticize their (or other) local, state, and federal governments. With this crucial question answered, the Palestinian is now free to focus on the pursuit of happiness.

Compared to these manifold benefits, and no drawbacks, consider how other paradigms respond to the Palestinian Question. Independence offers the countless frustrations of a start-up country, one which would be largely surrounded and pockmarked by a hostile country and without macroeconomic momentum. An Islamic state corrupts religion with secular power, converting what is pure into yet another victim to the adage "Absolute power corrupts absolutely." Without the stability of American statehood, every other paradigm invites subjugation of democratic processes, violations of due process, collapse of economic conditions, inadequacy of social services, and diversion of scarce resources to security. Of course, not all of these problems must necessarily manifest, but the risks are high that at least some of them will. Yet, what benefits are obtained, in terms of realizing Palestinian aspirations, by taking on these risks when American statehood achieves those aspirations without the risks?

As a Palestinian-majority state in the United States, Palestinians will be surrounded by evidence that their national aspirations have been fulfilled. The state's flag will be the Palestinian flag. State holidays will remember Palestinian heroes. A Palestinian-controlled unicameral or bicameral state legislature will pass laws that aim to better the lives of the people living in Palestine. Local police will evict and jail land trespassers. Local zoning boards will decide when, whether, and how to build roads and settlements. Local courts will ensure that the civil and criminal rights of all Palestinians are protected, regardless of their religion, ethnicity, or political opinions. Factories and office buildings will rise from the ruins of military occupation, as global capital pours into a politically-stable and economically-attractive environment. A Palestinian-American state will satisfy both the past century of nationalist aspirations and the next century of humanist aspirations. Dreams of life, liberty, and the pursuit of happiness will resonate in the souls of this generation of Palestinian youth.

Discrimination

Some may challenge the bucolic picture of a Palestinian nation nestled within an American haven. They may observe that even if it meets the three requirements of nationhood, the Palestinian people will still face discrimination that they wouldn't face in their own sovereign state. The three requirements of nationhood are self-determination, statehood, and national independence.

A Palestinian-American state achieves self-determination by virtue of a decision of its people to join America. Its statehood is respected by virtue of unambiguous and unchanging geographic boundaries and the rights of states in America's federal system. This division of power delegates broad authority to states for their local affairs. Finally, Palestinian national independence is coupled with American national independence. Because the Two Stars Plan makes Palestine part-and-parcel of the United States, the independence of one is the independence of the other.[2] The Two Stars Plan does not subjugate the Palestinians to the Americans. It makes the Palestinians Americans, while reserving to Palestinians their own cultural autonomy. Just as it was the destiny of Texas to continue to be independent as part of the United States, so it can be the destiny of Palestine.

Sadly, America still has problems with racial discrimination. What assurance do Palestinians have that their independence via America does not mean second-class citizenship?

Begin with the 350,000 Palestinians who already live in the United States. They are, by and large, well-off and happy. They are also largely invisible and frustrated by the media's negative reporting about Palestinians (usually linked to the word "terrorist"). When a Palestinian-American says they are from "near Jerusalem," it will generally be assumed they are Israeli and may often elicit sympathy or an offering of commiseration against Palestinians. When a Palestinian-American says they are from Ramallah, or simply Palestine, conversations generally end quickly. While Americans are typically quite knowledgeable about Israel, they are wholly ignorant of the Palestinian story. None of this, however, amounts to second-class citizenship. All of the frustrations and closeted identities will be relieved with American statehood for Palestine.

Under the Two Stars Plan, at least 3 million Palestinians will be added to the U.S. population. Overnight, the number of Palestinian-Americans will rise tenfold. After accounting for the new Israeli-Americans provided for in the Two Stars Plan, Palestinian-Americans will rise from being 5% as numerous as Jewish-Americans to being at least 25% as numerous. This is a huge increase in visibility that, coupled with the blanket media coverage that would accompany Palestine's

---

2. The U.S. is unusual in that newly-admitted states, such as Palestine, are admitted *on the same basis* as the original thirteen states that formed the country. Palestine really does become independent through America's independence. U.S. Supreme Court Justice Field described it this way in 1883 with regard to Illinois: "On her admission, she at once became entitled to and possessed of *all the rights of dominion and sovereignty* which belonged to the original states. She was admitted, and could be admitted, only on the same footing with them. The language of the act of admission is, 'on an equal footing with the original states in all respects whatever.' Equality of constitutional right and power is the condition of all the states of the Union, old and new." *Escanaba & Lake Michigan Transp. Co. v. City of Chicago*, 107 U.S. 678 (1883) (emphasis supplied) (citations omitted).

admission into the United States, all but guarantees an increasingly positive image of Palestinians in America.

America has had discrimination problems in the past, and continues to have them. What country doesn't? Where America rises above the rest of the world is in her aggressive determination to tackle discrimination head-on with laws, lawsuits, and thought-provoking media programming. Americans know they are now, or are on the verge of becoming, a majority-minority nation. In such a country, discrimination against any one minority is quickly viewed as potential discrimination against all minorities, and hence against the majority. This thought process helps to stamp out discrimination whenever it gets beyond the stage of being the isolated acts of "crazy fools."

Additional protection for Palestinian-Americans will flow from their two guaranteed seats in the powerful U.S. Senate and their four or more seats in the House of Representatives. If they work strategically, Palestinian Representatives and Senators can become members of powerful Congressional committees, and after time, the Chairmen. Finally, anti-Palestinian discrimination would be suicidal in the American state of Palestine, with its overwhelming Palestinian majority. Palestinians may be confident of first-class citizenship under the Two Stars Plan and its array of systematic protections. Over time, Americans will become as proud of Palestine as they are of Hawaii and Texas.

It should be remembered that the alternative to American statehood does not provide first-class citizenship outside of Palestine. Without American statehood, Palestinians will carry distinctive passports and will be surrounded by a hostile power. In an age of global travel, there will be no end to the security-based indignities that they will suffer, in large part because the Middle-East crisis will continue to fester and flare. A stump state littered with alien settlements and concrete corridors will not satisfy the next generation of Palestinian youth. As their frustration turns to violence, the world will continue to paint Palestinians with the terrorist brush. Global second-class citizenship is inevitable under such conditions. In contrast, the Two Stars Plan offers Palestinians first-class citizenship both domestically as well as globally.

Reparations

Palestinians have suffered a great deal of injustice in the last century. Palestinians will undoubtedly seek reparations for the harms they have suffered. Some Palestinians may feel that it will be easier for them to pursue reparations through the legal system of a Palestinian nation than as citizens of the United States. The opposite is more likely true. The recent success of German-Jewish families in obtaining compensation via the American legal system for theft of their property during World War II demonstrates this point.

It is never easy to obtain compensation for historical wrongs. It is especially difficult when the wrong-doer is a government. A key strategic point is identifying the best defendant. In the case of lost Palestinian lands, the problem began in the mid-1800s when communal estates were taken away from the great-great-grandparents of today's Palestinians by Ottoman land registration and tax laws. Legal niceties may have been complied with in some cases, and not in others. Can the Turkish successor to the Ottoman government be sued? Can legal actions be maintained against some of the Beirut, Damascus, and other remotely-located registered owners of the indigenous people's lands, many of who may not have properly paid for the vast estates they accumulated? Or perhaps the lawsuits should be directed against the Israeli organizations that purchased the absentee landlords' estates? Can valid title be obtained in the face of Ottoman laws prohibiting the sale of land to foreigners? If not, would the Zionist land-purchasing organizations then join those who sold the land to them and seek indemnification for any damages the Israeli organizations have to pay? What liability do the British have for their management of matters under the Palestine Mandate?

There are also reparation claims that arise from contemporary military conquests, settler encroachments, and government eminent-domain proceedings. Does Jordan share legal responsibility in the West Bank, and Egypt in the Gaza? Can settler organizations be sued instead of the government of Israel? What legal liability might the individual settler have? Does it matter if the motivation was religious or merely financial? Do legal doctrines such as adverse possession or fraudulent conveyance apply in this context?

Obtaining reparations for just the loss of Palestinian real estate over the last century will be a massively knotty legal problem. One must wisely choose the right defendants, the best applicable laws, and the winning litigation strategies. But progress can be made, as the successful efforts against Swiss Banks and German manufacturing companies showed, for wrongs perpetrated over a half century ago.

A legal judgment obtained in a U.S. court stands a better chance of being enforced against a defendant. The U.S. judicial system is over 200 years old, and that longevity has earned it substantial respect worldwide. In addition, many of the potential defendants have substantial assets in the United States. It is a great deal easier to execute a U.S. court's judgment against U.S.-based assets.

Under article 4, section 1 of the U.S. Constitution, each American state must give "full faith and credit" to the "judicial proceedings" of any other state, subject to any nationwide limitations that the U.S. Congress may prescribe. As states in the U.S., both Israeli and Palestinian judicial rulings would be binding in each other's states, and in any other American state, provided the judicial rulings were valid in terms of jurisdiction and applicable law. For example, suppose a settler in the West Bank wrongfully bulldozed a Palestinian's olive grove and erected a trailer camp. Aside from any criminal sanctions, the settler could be sued in a Palestinian civil court, as it would clearly have jurisdiction over the matter. A Palestinian court judgment for damages, such as the lost economic value of the olive grove, would have to be enforced by an Israeli court against the Israeli assets of the settler, and by a Florida court if he moved to Florida or had assets there. This demonstrates the superiority of American statehood in pursuing Palestinian claims for reparations.

Right of Return

Chapter 2 described how the Palestinian Right of Return could be satisfied within the Two Stars Plan. First, Palestinians who can prove they were born in Israeli-Palestinian space, no matter where they currently reside, will be granted U.S. citizenship in the Congressional legislation that accepted Israel and Palestine as new states (and thereby made all of their current residents U.S. citizens). Second, the same legislation would grant U.S. citizenship to all lineally-descended family members (such as grandchildren) of Palestinians born in Israeli-Palestinian space, but displaced as stateless persons to foreign refugee camps or non-citizenship-granting countries. For example, suppose a Palestinian man was born in Jaffa, left in 1948 for a Lebanese refugee camp, and there had a son who currently is a non-citizen resident of Kuwait. Under the Two Stars Plan, that son, along with his wife and children, would be made a U.S. citizen upon the filing of the appropriate documentation. This is every bit as much of a Right of Return as would be granted by an independent Palestine.

It may be countered that the legislation described above would not cover a Right of Return for Palestinians who have citizenship in other countries. While that is true, the citizenship needs of these persons are significantly less urgent than those of stateless persons. As noted in Chapter 2, a new Right of Return visa category could be created as part of the statehood legislation to accommodate citizens of other countries who want to immigrate to Palestine. This visa would require settlement in Palestine, which would eventually allow it to mature into a grant of U.S. citizenship. The new state of Palestine, which is already one of the ten most densely-populated places in the world, will have its hands full accommodating the 1–2 million stateless Palestinians that will become automatic U.S. citizens (and may well decide to reside in a Palestinian town). By limiting the granting of Right of Return visas to about 70,000 per year (reflecting the level of immigration into Israel from its similarly-sized Diaspora), the new U.S. state of

Palestine can do a better job of helping to integrate the million plus stateless Palestinians who will likely arrive en masse as U.S. citizens.

Culture

Palestinians are no more willing to lose their culture under an American cultural tsunami than are the Israelis. They also have nothing to fear on this account, as was shown for the Israelis in Chapter 5. American culture will not succeed where it is not welcomed. This is why Starbucks went out of business in Israel. No one wanted to pay sky-high prices for coffee in a place that knows coffee like a Bedouin knows camels.

It may be observed that as more of a blank-slate economy, compared to neighboring Israel, Palestine could be more susceptible to "economic colonization" by U.S. franchises and media. This argument underestimates the steadfastness of Palestinian culture and the cleverness of Palestinian people. Neither centuries of Ottoman influence nor decades of Egyptian, Israeli, Jordanian, Lebanese, and Syrian oppression have extinguished—or even dampened—the vibrant Palestinian culture, which is strongly anchored around the ancient towns of their land. The Palestinians can undoubtedly be counted on to adopt the good structures that they see but to infuse those structures with their own cultural content. Hence, the Palestinians may like American marketing methods, but they will use those methods to market products that meet local needs. They may like American media offerings, but they will add to those channels ones that provide engaging Palestinian content.

Palestinians will be in charge of local school boards, zoning committees, and state regulatory offices. There will be ample power and means to ensure that local commercial practices are consistent with local cultural sensitivities. At the same time, by welcoming mainland U.S. companies and franchises to Palestine, huge business opportunities will open up to the benefit of the local economy. There is a lot of rebuilding to do in Palestine. A few Home Depots and a local Wal-Mart would be a welcome sight for thousands of Palestinian homeowners and apartment dwellers.

It is not an easy decision for a people to entrust its future onto any particular path. The soul weighs as heavily with concerns for one's grandchildren as it does with obligations to one's grandparents. Such choices cause grown men to ask, what would their fathers do? Mature women pray for a guide to their children's happiness. History separates winners from losers with bright yellow lines, but the future is as murky as the fog-shrouded night.

Indecision is a sad decision. This option would disappoint ancestors, for they did not commit themselves to raise a generation to sit like a potted plant. Parents and grandparents sacrifice and suffer so that a new generation can stand tall. Lying down flat with indecision, at a critical juncture and in a tumultuous time, invites the future to plow over the present, leaving tread marks in its wake. Even if the right choice is not clear, a clear choice is right. It is important to stand and be counted not once but thrice. People must choose once with pride for themselves. People must choose a second time with gratitude for all those who came before them and struggled so that they may be here. Finally, people must choose a third time for all those who come next—they will rise as high in their life as the fulcrum is positioned between this generation and the next. Postponing action moves the fulcrum to the future and limits the next generation's lift. Decide now, and decide wisely, and the fulcrum is set close to this generation. Future generations will rise high thanks to the actions taken today.

Choosing wisely between standalone statehood and American statehood cannot be too tough. Chapters 2 and 3 demonstrated convincingly that *only* the Two Stars Plan systematically solves the long-running problem of Middle-East peace. This chapter went even further, showing issue-by-issue that even uniquely Palestinian concerns are far more satisfactorily resolved within an integral, well-respected American state than within a perforated, grindingly-poor start-up state. With the Two Stars Plan, the Palestinians move into the future, both structurally, in terms of multi-state union-hood, and culturally, via a safe socioeconomic matrix. The Two Stars Plan enables the Palestinian identity to blossom. Any other solution is a step backwards, into twentieth-century nationhood, into Bantustan apartheid, into insecurity and injustice and violence. How does a garden bloom with bullets tearing up its soil and displacing its seed? It doesn't. A Golden Age of Palestinian culture will only occur if the people are willing, collectively, to make the choice and vote for American-Palestinian statehood.

Two standalone states in one Israeli-Palestinian space makes as much sense as two men sitting on a wobbly stool. They will fight, and one will fall. He who falls will pull the stool's legs until gravity rules. Or maybe it's more like a stepstool, whimsically expecting Palestinian satisfaction on the step of an Israeli seat. The Two Stars Plan, on the other hand, places a couch where there was but a stool. Each man may sit in his corner, and may even visit the other's side. There are no obvious barriers on a couch, and yet no one in good form occupies more than his half. There is nothing to fight for and no place to fall.

Couches are not loveseats, and no one expects affection among peoples with reasons to hate. Nevertheless, an American statehood couch, in a single Israeli-Palestinian space, makes a lot more sense than a standalone stool. It took the American South and North more than a century to feel affection for each other, and some animosity still remains. But the people of each region are happy. They are free to pursue life-goals and their cultures blossom, nestled in the safety of constitutional protection and historical pride. So too will it be for the Palestinian people.

There is no obligation to love neighbors, just as Alabamans and Yanks have their contrary ways. The obligation is to respect the rights of others as one's own rights are respected. It is this mutuality of respect that the U.S. Constitution, and U.S. statehood, ensures.

It is the decision of American statehood that bellows out from the future. It is this decision that gives to children a birthright of a robust Palestinian culture. It is this decision that best respects all of the suffering and sacrifices made in the name of Palestinian nationhood. It is this decision that makes the Palestinian national identity a beacon of pride, prescience, and prosperity. With the foresight to achieve statehood via union with America, this Palestinian generation will have done right by those no longer breathing this planet's air. This generation with have done righter still by those yet dormant in our eyes, waiting for their chance to blossom before the sun.

7

Arab Considerations

Whoever marries my mother, I will call him uncle.

—Arabic Proverb

Submit, O my soul, to the decision of destiny,
And use the time in my return and repentance.
Do not think back to a time that has passed,
When I received favors long gone, and reproaches.
Address now the gracious master,
Who was inspired with the success of the Qur'an,
Who is noble in end and origin,
The lion of the flock, the full moon of the assembly,
Upon whom victory descends, as
The revelation descends by means of the holy spirit.

—Abu Abdallah al-Khatib, translated from Arabic

While the future of Palestinian statehood is up to Palestinians to decide, the opinions of Arab brethren worldwide are important. From these brethren have come decades of moral, financial and intellectual support. The general view will be that whatever is best for the Palestinian people is all that the Arab World wants. However, Arab views are not homogenous. There will be questions about U.S. intentions. There will be concerns about the impact upon Arab unity. There will be second-guessing of Palestinian interests. This chapter endeavors to identify the uniquely Arab considerations that arise from the Two Stars Plan. If Arab World sentiment applauds the wisdom of a Palestinian-American state, it will facilitate Palestinian decision-making. Based on a fair assessment of Arab interests, that applause should be loud and long.

Pan-Arabism Can Transcend Borders

At one time it was thought that nationalism was contrary to Pan-Arabism. That view died rather quickly, especially when Libya, Egypt, and Syria went their separate ways. Instead, the prevailing thinking is that Pan-Arabism transcends national borders. Indeed, by strengthening local Arab communities with local infrastructure projects, nation-states have helped to build a stronger Arab World. The ideology of Pan-Arab unity is more attractive on the shoulders of a stronger Arab World. Consequently, separate Arab political entities are building blocks for Pan-Arabism, not obstacles.

The Arab World's challenge to the Two Stars Plan is this: does it augment or detract from Pan-Arabism? Does it subtract three million or more Palestinians from the Arab World or does it constitute one of the mightiest building blocks ever in the Pan-Arab dream?

At present, the Palestinian people cannot contribute much to the Arab World. After all, they have only a proto-country, are largely stateless, and are fighting for their survival. Consequently, by merging Palestine with the United States, the Arab World is not losing anything, since the current situation is so marginal. On the other hand, as a vibrant American state—and the first Arab-majority American state—the Palestinian people will make a huge contribution to the strength of Pan-Arabism. It is no small thing to achieve elected representation in the highest corridors of power of the world's most powerful nation. Overnight, a Palestinian-American state makes America itself part of the Arab World.

Arab World leaders from Saudi Arabia to Egypt now have a cause to celebrate. Here is a plan that adds to their peoples' greatness while taking nothing away.

From Paris to Beirut, Pan-Arab organizations, aboveground or in hiding, and in a hundred or more venues, must also pay attention. It is admittedly strange to think that union with America is good for the cause. But straight lines often lead to wrong places, and the circuitous path is often more wise. The Two Stars Plan converts one of America's states into an Arab-majority state, quickly and peacefully, with no further limitations on the growth of pan-Arabism. How else could such an astonishing feat be accomplished? Given the reality of American power and influence, there is no other way to propel the cause of Pan-Arab identity faster than from the platform of an Arab-majority American state. This is especially so considering that it will be fueled with ample working capital and a diversity of multimedia outlets.

Moral Obligation to Support Palestinians' Best Interests

Upon the century-long suffering of the Palestinian people has been built one important pillar of Arab world unity. While the modern world gives sovereigns much to disagree about, all Arab countries have found common ground in support for the self-determination rights of the Palestinian people. Now it is time to show that Arab unity pays valuable dividends when the critical moment arrives. By uniting behind the Palestinian people's decision to become an equal state in the United States, the Arab World will satisfy an important moral obligation to support their brethren's best interests.

Of course, there is an opportunity for Arab thought to debate endlessly the pros and cons of Palestinian merger with America. But such debate does not serve the Palestinians' best interests. They have already suffered through the debates of Arab nationalism, having been torn into Jordanian and Egyptian domains only to be lost in battle a few years later.[1] They have already lost generation after generation while much of the rest of the Arab World advances to higher levels of social, cultural, and technological development. They have already tried struggling as a stump-state, battling for a real state, and suffocating in a refugee state. The Palestinian people have a right to try something new, dramatic, and highly promising. They have a right to try to develop their culture and national identity as an equal part of the United States.

This is a precious opportunity for the entire Arab World to unite behind Palestine in its moment of decision. The Arab World can help most by encouraging Palestinians to be confident in their decision and by comforting Americans that they, too, at long last, have made the right choice. From the Arab World we need the Two Stars Plan to become *Alam al-mithral*, a shared dream of goodwill, among so many millions of brothers that it becomes real.

Arabs everywhere have always shared the Palestinians' dream. Their support is counted on more now than ever before. They must help realize the Palestinian dream, not as a figment state at the bottom of the world economic ladder, but as a citadel state at the top. This citadel state is not a fortress but a storehouse of one of the most beautiful strains of Arab culture and thought. Its umbilical connection to America ensures that the Palestinian way of life will grow abundantly, bearing sweet-tasting fruit for Arab people everywhere.

---

1. There is evidence that King Abdullah of Jordan actually wanted to prevent the formation of a Palestinian state west of the Jordan, and for that reason joined the 1948 Arab League war against Israel. Jordan did later annex the West Bank, and generally offered passports and citizenship to Palestinians. However, after losing the West Bank and Jerusalem to Israel in the 1967 Six Day War, Jordan never regained its enthusiasm for its original plan. The Israel-Jordan peace treaty accepts as their border the eastern demarcation of Palestine (including the Jordan River) that the British surveyed at the start of their mandate in 1920. Former Jordanian occupied territory west of this line is now reserved for the Palestinian state, as was the UN's original intention in 1947.

Neighbors Will Benefit from Stability

Completely aside from the Arab World's interest in helping Palestinians, the Two Stars Plan must also be assessed from the standpoint of its effect on geopolitical stability in the Middle East.[2] This part of the world is unstable today. There are too many weapons in too small a space, with too many tripwires about. Israel and her Arab neighbors have fought five wars in fifty-five years, including the ongoing *intifada*. The huge, nuclear-capable Israeli army must remain on hot standby so long as Arab enemies surround it. Neighboring Arab countries, on the other hand, must maintain large standing armies in the hope of an opportunity to reclaim lost land and in defense against losing more. On top of all this, the millions of dissatisfied Palestinians spread throughout Lebanon, Syria, Jordan and Gaza constitute a multitude of roving tripwires. Nature will suck them into any geopolitical vacuum. Israeli and Arab defense forces must also control the Palestinian masses, creating numerous insults in the process, any one of which may flare into local or regional violence. The instability of stateless masses, compounded by the instability of hostile borders, creates the probability of violent conflict. No wonder economic development stalls.

With the Two Stars Plan, the Palestinian tripwires will be cut along with the endless kilometers of barbed wire keeping them where they don't want to be. Stateless Palestinians will be welcomed as U.S. citizens, free to live in Palestine, Israel, or the rest of the United States. Armies will no longer be needed to manage huge refugee populations. This major source of instability will be transformed into a positive economic engine for growth, which is a source of great stability.

Under the Two Stars Plan, there is no longer any need for large armies to face each other across the Golan Heights, the Bekaa Valley, or the Jordan River. The U.S. is not going after more land—the occupation headaches would far outweigh any conceivable rewards. Indeed, the only argument for the U.S. itself to support the Two Stars Plan is that the hassles and costs of incorporating Israel and Palestine are outweighed by the risks to world peace of chronic instability in Israeli-Palestinian space. However, there is no comparable level of chronic instability in Lebanon, Syria, Jordan, or Egypt. No other country in the Middle East can claim the dubious moniker of having caused the entire world gut-wrenching angst for nearly a century.

---

2. Palestinians have long been a political football between Egypt and Jordan, and among other Arab States, at least from the time Egypt and Jordan sponsored rival National Councils and Congresses in September 1948. One was in Gaza and the other in Amman, one was devoted to sovereign independence and the other to incorporation into Jordan. When the Palestinian football flew, the Palestinian masses followed, contributing to the huge refugee populations and regional instability of today.

With Israel and Palestine merged into America, its neighbors can rest as peacefully as do Canada and Mexico along the thousands of kilometers of border they share with the United States. Even more exciting is that the stability of a U.S. border will enable Lebanon, Syria, Jordan, and Egypt to experience the same kind of economic boom that Mexico and Canada enjoy. Regional stability, expansion of pan-Arab influence, and a better quality of life for Palestinians are three independent reasons for the Arab World to support Palestinian statehood in the U.S.

8

European Interests

If we do not find anything pleasant, at least we shall find something new.

—Voltaire, *Candide*, 1759

In diplomacy, form is substance. Benign geopolitical moves have been rendered intolerable through arrogance, while consultation and consensus have paved highways through hell. Being a relatively young country, America has not learned as well as Europe the rights and wrongs of global discourse. She is best analogized to a precocious but inconsistent youngster. In one decade she'll pleasantly astound the world with the genius of multilateral institutions such as the UN, the World Bank, and NATO. In another decade she'll profoundly disappoint the world with brash, unilateral actions such as disavowing global treaties covering greenhouse emissions, international criminals, and atomic weapons.

At times, America no doubt feels like a Gulliver, being pinned down against her will by dozens of smaller countries. Yet it is the responsibility of a superpower to charm the Lilliputians into more productive endeavors. Brash unilateralism breeds increasing resistance just as air friction increases with the fourth power of speed. Sometimes America may find herself having to agree to something that she does not really believe is right. The astute response in this situation is the tactical retreat—sign the treaty, internally evaluate what went wrong with diplomacy, and then use more creative diplomatic approaches to win the endgame. Al Capone was wrong that people pay more attention to nice words and a gun than to nice words alone. The gun just gets you the wrong kind of attention, drowning out the message of the nice words entirely.

America's power makes the world want to oppose her. Yet that opposition becomes dangerous only when left unchanneled. After World War II, the U.S. was relatively more powerful than today. At that time, her economy produced 50% of world GNP, and all other countries were in ruins. In those days she designed her own multilateral bindings, ones that would not adversely constrain, and made the effort to persuade the world to adopt those bindings as an invention they co-owned. Though stricken seriously with polio, Roosevelt traveled halfway around the world to Yalta at the peak of America's power, demonstrating grace in victory and making multilateralism the new world order. Thus, the UN was formed, but it would not stop America's self-defense efforts. An anti-nuclear regime fell into place, but it focused on non-proliferation rather than on American and Soviet stockpiles.

The price of power is patience. Without patience, power will be applied frequently and unilaterally, thereby sowing the seeds of resistance that can ultimately strangle and destroy even great world powers. By paying out patience, however, power can persevere, as resistance will lack momentum. Patience, on the other hand, does not mean acquiescence. Power abhors a vacuum and enemies will grow fat on whatever a power leaves behind. For a superpower, it is all about timing and deft use of diplomacy. Patiently bring all key constituencies onboard before taking forceful action, but neither wait too long nor fail in diplomacy. If diplomatic failure is imminent, redefine the game and improve diplomacy the next time around. Exercising superpower status is like playing poker and getting to draw three cards when everyone else draws one. It doesn't guarantee a winning hand, but it makes bluffing much easier. In other words, power fuels diplomacy while diplomacy preserves power. When power bypasses diplomacy, both are rapidly squandered and spent.

The U.S. must realize that Europe has a strong interest in Middle-East peace. In addition, Europe has strong concerns regarding the size and number of American footprints around the world. The fact that Europe has no legal right to contest the Two Stars Plan is irrelevant. She is a diplomatic player on the world stage. She is as connected to the powder keg of Middle-East affairs as is America. If she is bypassed, resistance will arise. If she is included, the power of the solution will be enhanced.

The way to include Europe in the Two Stars Plan is to positively demarche the concept with her from the very beginning. In quiet rooms, present the pros and cons, the interests and counter-interests. Listen to the European perspectives. She is, in fact, the world model at creating a union from a multiplicity of separate states. She will have much to say and contribute to an optimally-fashioned Two Stars Plan.

Geography Does Not Imply Hegemony

At first blush, the appearance of two new American states at Europe's geographic doorstep will seem troubling. This perception should be acknowledged and treated for what it is—a mere geographic perception without practical significance. Geography does not imply hegemony.

Consider the last two American states: Hawaii and Alaska. While the first lies near the South Pacific, and the second abuts Russia, neither contributed to U.S. hegemony in those areas. The U.S. traded in Asia before it annexed Hawaii, so it was not trade that influenced the annexation. Subsequently, the U.S. has achieved no material advantages in Asia vis-à-vis the Japanese or the Chinese from having this island state. As for Alaska and Russia, their proximate geography has greater importance to migrating polar bears than to movers and shakers.

This is not to say that geography may not have military or commercial importance, but only that it does not necessarily imply the same. It is appropriate to look to Alaska and Hawaii as examples in order to see what can or cannot be implied from U.S. statehood for Israel and Palestine. Should Europe be concerned with any commercial or military advantages that might accrue to the U.S. from its acquiring a sovereign toehold in the Middle East?

It is untenable to argue that the U.S. requires Israel or Palestine to field military forces. There is not even any reason to think that such bases would make a material difference in a U.S. war effort. As has been amply demonstrated in Afghanistan, Kuwait, and Iraq, the U.S. is already able to project its military power without great strain. Israeli or Palestinian bases do not bring any material advantage over the current approach of using aircraft carriers, air-to-air refueling, and treaty-based arrangements with a multiplicity of other countries, including U.K. assets such as Diego Garcia. The battles around the periphery of the Arabian Peninsula were accomplished swiftly with minimal loss of life. What more can one ask for?

It is also unbelievable to conceive that the U.S. wants Israel and Palestine to become states so that annexation would extend, domino-like, to oil-rich states such as Saudi Arabia and Iraq. Their oil makes up a minority of U.S. imports and is available at a modest cost. Advances in hydrogen fuel cells are on the cusp of making oil less and less important. It would be as irrational to annex these countries as it would be to build a castle on the beach when the same view is available from hotel rooms rented by the day. No American could possibly believe his or her country would ever behave so irrationally as to absorb 30 million Iraqis as American citizens.[1]

Aside from annexation or military benefits, some Europeans may perceive a commercial advantage accruing to America by virtue of having two Middle-East

---

1. To be sure, many Americans will be hesitant about the Two Stars Plan for similar reasons, as they relate to 6 million Israelis and 3 million Palestinians. However, in the case of the Two Stars Plan, what is achieved in exchange is rare and unique: world peace. No other country in the world presents such a compelling and long-running threat to global stability.

states. This too seems unlikely. Certainly, Israel will not open any commercial doors in the Arab World, and the U.S. is already Israel's largest source of both imports and exports. As for Palestine, the U.S. may well benefit from the business and professional links Palestinians have established throughout the Arab World. However, this is small potatoes compared to the mega-contracts Europe and the United States compete for most vigorously.

Decisions about international pipelines, new fleets of jet aircraft, and massive construction projects are not going to be based on Palestinian rolodexes. These major commercial contracts will be let in the same way as they have always been, based on value comparisons between competing bids and government-to-government lobbying efforts. The U.S. did not lose many of these contracts because its Apache helicopters were being used to bomb Palestinian motorcades, and it will not win many of them because it has given 3 million Palestinians U.S. passports. Big business does not usually march to a humanitarian tune.

Even if the added geography is nevertheless seen to benefit the U.S. in some way, it must be remembered that a much greater advantage flows to the Palestinian and Israeli peoples, as well as to the entire world. By bringing peace to an area of the world that has seen far too little of it, and by defusing at least one major justification for terrorism, the Two Stars Plan makes the whole world a better place. Europe's leading role in matters of humanitarian assistance demonstrates its noble willingness to incur costs for the greater good. Here, too, Europeans may say to themselves, "Even if the U.S. gains, or if we lose a bit, it is worth it to make the world a safer place."

EU Expansion Is a Counterweight

The expansion of the EU is another factor to consider in light of the Two Stars Plan. It has recently been expanded from fifteen to twenty-five countries, including the Mediterranean countries of Malta and Cypress. Turkey is in queue to be considered for membership. Why not include Israel and Palestine as EU members instead of American states?

The simple answer is that membership in the EU is only open to European countries. By geographic convention, Israel and Palestine are in Asia, not Europe. Perhaps this restriction could be eliminated in recognition of the fact that newly admitted Cypress is but 400 kilometers from Israel. Other unambiguously European countries, such as Russia, lie eastward of Israel and Palestine. Even Turkey is spoken of as straddling Europe and Asia. Furthermore, Israel is a member of several European organizations. Will the Europeans let reality rule over geography and admit Israel and Palestine into the EU? Probably not.

Europeans are rightly concerned with integrating the countries they have just absorbed in their largest expansion ever.[2] This would be an inopportune time to open the door to expansion even beyond European frontiers. How could admission be limited to Israel and Palestine without also considering the Northern African lands that once formed part of the Roman Empire?

In addition, a European location is the least part of the entry criteria for the EU. Applying countries must also show detailed political and economic ability "to take on the obligations of membership" and demonstrate "possession of the necessary administrative structures." The EU's Amsterdam Treaty further stipulates that eligibility for membership depends on respect for the principles on which the EU itself is founded: "liberty, democracy, respect for human rights and fundamental freedoms, and the rule of law." The inability of Romania, Bulgaria, and Turkey to meet these criteria has led to a deferral of their applications. It is most doubtful that Israel or Palestine, for different reasons, would succeed any sooner.

It is not realistic to think of EU membership as the needed near-term, out-of-the-box solution to the Middle-East crisis. But, it should be comforting to Europeans that, even as the U.S. expands into the Mediterranean Basin via Israeli and Palestinian states, the EU is expanding just 400 kilometers offshore. In other words, the EU's expansion has preemptively met the American expansion, in a geographic sense. The EU presence in this area will grow dramatically once the admission process is complete for Turkey, perhaps just a few years from now. Consequently, the geopolitical situation is not one of a growing America and a static Europe. To the contrary, the EU is growing much more rapidly than is the U.S.

All Alternatives Are Worse

Logic aside, American states in the Eastern Mediterranean may leave a sour taste in some European mouths. There is just something odd about American territory outside the Western Hemisphere. Yet, this is not a neatly-contained world. We all must improvise to solve the problems at hand.

As explained in Chapter 2, the problems of the Middle East cannot realistically be solved by the so-called two-state roadmap: two sovereign states on one

---

2. The European Union just expanded from fifteen to twenty-five members. The EU has enlarged five times since its foundation in 1957. It began life with six members (Belgium, France, Germany, Italy, Luxembourg, and the Netherlands), increased to nine in 1973 (Denmark, Ireland, and the U.K.), to ten in 1981 (Greece), to twelve in 1986 (Portugal and Spain), and to fifteen in 1995 (Austria, Finland and Sweden). The newest members, approved in 2003, are Cyprus, Malta, Hungary, the Czech Republic, Poland, Estonia, Latvia, Lithuania, Slovenia, and Slovakia.

integrated piece of land. This is a bandage that gives the impression of progress but actually only hides festering wounds. The next flashpoint may be Jerusalem, or the Right of Return, or Israeli maintenance of long-standing settlements, or simply the growing disparity in wealth between two crushingly-close neighbors. None of these flashpoints are even dealt with under the so-called roadmap, but they are all definitively resolved by the Two Stars Plan.

It would be possible for Europe, and America, to string the Israelis and Palestinians along for decades on end with dead-end solutions. Situations like this exist worldwide. Instead of solving the problem, experts manage the problem, keeping it from exploding across too many international borders or causing too great a level of television shock. Yet, the world owes Israelis and Palestinians better than that.

When Europe began to encourage thousands of Jewish settlers onto a well-settled land, they acquired some responsibility for today's situation. When the Allies dismembered the Ottoman Empire, they acquired some responsibility for its scattered peoples. When European and American governments did little to halt the Holocaust, they acquired some responsibility for ensuring that a "never-again" safe haven exists. For all of these reasons, Europeans must stand up and be counted among the supporters of Two Stars for Peace. Even if it is not a plan that would have emanated from European councils, it is a plan that solves the problem better than any other. Because Europeans share responsibility for the problem, the right thing to do is to vigorously support its most comprehensive solution.

9

International Issues

If the UN expects to be able to partition Palestine without forces to help maintain order and to enforce partition, its thinking is most unrealistic and its efforts will be in vain.

—Robert Macatee, American Consul General in Jerusalem, 1947

We have now asked and answered almost every possible question relating to the merger of Israeli and Palestinian states into the United States. By this point, every reasonable person must be in agreement with the Two Stars for Peace Plan. Agreement is sometimes accompanied by second-level confusion, and so it may be here. For example, "This makes sense, but isn't it like imperialism—and isn't that bad?" or perhaps, "This is a good solution, but doesn't it need to be adopted by the United Nations?" or even, "I like the Two Stars Plan, but won't it take a global treaty to pull it off?" The purpose of this chapter is to resolve these intellectual and legal questions.

No Neo-isms Apply

When people decide with free will to join another country, colonialism and imperialism do not exist. Free will, though, is notoriously difficult to pin down. If what seemed to be free will was actually manipulated by another country for its benefit, then colonialism or imperialism would exist. Consequently, the key question is: why would America support merging Israeli and Palestinian states into the United States? If it is being done so that Middle-Eastern peoples can be dominated for the benefit of North Americans, then this is imperialism. But there is absolutely no evidence of this. If it is being done for altruistic purposes, such as a better quality of life in the view of the Middle-Eastern peoples, then it is just good international development. This, in fact, is what has been documented in every chapter of this book. What seems like free will really will be free will. The labels of imperialism and colonialism do not in any way apply.

America has no policy of extending herself through the vehicle of U.S. state-hood. Indeed, she has not added a state in fifty years. Americans in general will not be eager to absorb these two states, but they will certainly be willing to do so in the interests of peace, stability, and responsibility. American trade will not particularly benefit from the Two Stars Plan. Her military will not be made stronger. The only advantage America reaps from this plan is that a divertive preoccupation of her for-eign policy, Middle-East peace, will be resolved. Speculatively, the Two Stars Plan may also dampen enthusiasm for terrorism worldwide. Such benign motivations cannot support a finding of colonialism or imperialism. Instead, it is what it looks like: a pragmatic people (Americans) applying a practical solution (U.S. statehood) to help geopolitically trapped people (Israelis and Palestinians) out of a problem-atic situation (two peoples, one land). No-*isms* apply.

The UN's Role

Whenever we hear about Middle-East peace plans there seems to be UN resolu-tion numbers in the background. How can the Two Stars Plan be implemented in the face of all these UN resolutions? Is a new, final UN resolution required? What if it gets hijacked or blackballed?

Literally dozens of United Nations resolutions have been adopted relating to Israel and Palestine, commencing with General Assembly Resolution 181 calling, in 1947, for the partition of Palestine into Jewish and Arab states, plus an inter-nationalized Jerusalem district. The vast majority of these resolutions have been ignored, commencing with much of Resolution 181 itself. The jigsaw-puzzle Resolution 181 partition lines are no longer realistic or relied upon by the Palestinian leadership. Instead, a much more useful demarcation is the border already accepted by the Palestinian Authority, coupled with East Jerusalem.

The UN has had great difficulty making progress in the Middle East. Rowing against the current of U.S. and Israeli public opinion on the subject of Israel has proven to be impractical. Nevertheless, it is still possible for the UN to establish a critical role for itself under the Two Stars Plan. This role would be true to its humanitarian mission and enable it to be counted among the contributors to a just and lasting Middle-East peace.

Shortly after adopting its Partitioning Resolution, the General Assembly reacted to the melee it occasioned (a multi-country invasion, general warfare, eth-nic cleansing, and mass hysteria) by adopting Resolution 194 on December 11th, 1948:

> Resolves that the refugees wishing to return to their homes and live at
> peace with their neighbors should be permitted to do so at the earliest

practicable date, and that compensation should be paid for the property of those choosing not to return and for loss of or damage to property which, under principles of international law or in equity, should be made good by the Governments or authorities responsible.

The UN could contribute meaningfully to the Two Stars Plan by offering to set up a Palestine Economic Claims Adjustment Forum (PECAF). The role of PECAF would be to arrive at equitable compensation decisions in accordance with UNGA Resolution 194. This would go a long way toward reducing Palestinian disappointment with the world body and, at the same time, removing a major potential irritant in the Israeli, Palestinian, and U.S. federal court systems. If the UN made this proposal in a timely fashion, it is probable that the U.S. Congress could incorporate it into its statehood legislation and even grant to it exclusive jurisdiction over claims that pre-date 1950. The U.S. Congress could also allocate to PECAF a total sum of money for its disbursement amongst all claimants, similar to what was done with the World Trade Center Victims Fund.

It is important for the UN to help maintain respect for international law. This is why it should be cautious about adopting unenforceable resolutions. Nevertheless, the UN can step forward on a good footing by adopting a new resolution that:

- supports U.S. statehood for Israel and Palestine, in accordance with the wishes of their people, and deems such a solution to have satisfied and superceded all previous UN resolutions bearing on Israel and Palestine; and

- establishes PECAF and proposes it to have exclusive and comprehensive jurisdiction over claims arising from UNGA Resolution 194 in exchange for not less than $1 billion of U.S. funding.

The prospect of a new UN resolution brings with it the possibility of an unknown fate, similar to the meandering path of American-requested UN resolutions relating to alleged Iraqi weapons of mass destruction. However, as discussed in Chapter 8, patience is the price of power, and style is substance. Given the right attention to diplomacy, and the bushel-full of merits in favor of the Two Stars Plan, a straightforward UN resolution is achievable along the lines described above. Such a resolution would keep the international law books clear, while also helping to rebuild respect for UN resolutions as evidence of international law.

While the funding obligation rests upon the U.S., the recommended UN resolutions are really in its best interest. In this way, the legal "title" of its two new states is unclouded. In addition, rather than having to deal with the sticky wicket of pre-1950 compensation claims, it can refer all such matters to the UN. The savings in terms of court backlog, hard feelings, and potential U.S. liability as the successor sovereign is well worth the $1 billion of funding to cement the PECAF arrangement.[1]

With the best of intentions, the UN helped create the Middle-East mess. As resolution piled on top of resolution, the UN's credibility sank under the load of paper and debate. Now there is an opportunity to achieve justice and to help restore the UN's good name. Step one is to accept the Two Stars Plan as satisfaction of its past fifty years of resolutions, including the Partition Mandate. Step two is to accept tribunal responsibility for the adjustment and disbursement of claims for lost refugee property in the aftermath of the partition. In this way, the UN will have literally made good on its intentions of fifty-five years ago and will have helped move the world forward under the rule of law.

Will It Take a Treaty?

The Two Stars Plan can be implemented without any new treaty. The reason for this is that each of the entities involved will be making a bilateral relationship with the United States. What makes the whole solution work, though, is that each of these three bilateral arrangements occur in parallel.

Consider first Israel and Palestine. Each may use her sovereign power to accept a conditional Congressional invitation to statehood. Once Congress ratifies that acceptance by confirming that the necessary preconditions are in place, American statehood is in place. From that moment, politics and government proceed in accordance with the new Israeli and Palestinian state constitutions.

As for the UN, Congress may, as a bilateral matter, offer conditional funding for a Palestinian refugee-claims-adjustment tribunal. It is then up to the UN to ensure its General Assembly and/or Security Council passes the needed resolutions. Once this is done, the resolution vesting exclusive claims-adjustment authority in a UN tribunal funded by the U.S. constitutes binding international law. If Palestine does not yet have a formal UN vote at this time, it would be quite important for its representative to otherwise signal its acceptance on behalf of the Palestinian people. Nothing further, such as an international treaty, is required because of the broad global participation in this uber-resolution.

---

1. It is worth recalling that at the time the U.S. annexed Texas and paid out many millions of dollars to both Texas and Mexico in connection therewith, she was just emerging from the worst economic depression in her history, which began in 1837 and lasted into the 1840s. Clearly, the value associated with peace-building that supported merger with Texas was deemed well worth the substantial cash outlay, even in a time of unprecedented economic hardship.

10

Practical Steps and a Timeline

Begin to weave and God will give you thread.

—German proverb

This final chapter offers a pragmatic, sequential set of steps for implementing the Two Stars Plan. Certain sample and historical documents are provided as appendices. It is not the purpose of this chapter to presume to know precisely how Israeli and Palestinian states will merge into the United States. It is, however, the goal to outline what needs to be done for success and to encourage the reader to adopt a brisk timeline for its completion.

Grassroots Organizations

Two Stars for Peace is a social movement. All such movements begin with the people. Nothing can be started until individuals, such as the readers of this book, help organize local groups to educate others about Two Stars for Peace. The adage "Think globally, act locally" applies perfectly to this cause. Just a few people can touch all 300 million Americans, Israelis, and Palestinians in a very short period of time. The story of the invention of chess tells how.

The inventor of chess so pleased the Chinese emperor that he was promised anything he wanted as a reward. He asked for just one grain of rice, doubled per day, for each of the sixty-four squares on the chessboard. The emperor smiled at the man's humility and granted his wish. After eight days the inventor had received a grand total of 255 grains of rice.[1] All of Beijing was laughing. After sixteen days, he had about 64,000 grains of rice.[2] He was no longer able to count them so precisely, but they weighed in at a modest 2 kilograms. All of China was now bellowing and guffawing. The man who could have had a palace had

---

1. 1+2+4+8+16+32+64+128=255
2. 250+500+1000+2000+4000+8000+16,000+32,000=64,000

accepted two kilos of rice instead! After crossing the third row of the chessboard, though, the inventor had now acquired a quite respectable 500 kilos of rice—half a metric ton.[3] He now had more rice than all but the wealthiest princes, and people started to hold their breath. Indeed, at that point, he had about 15 million grains of rice.

If we imagine each grain as one person converted to the Two Stars for Peace cause, there would certainly be very close to a critical mass of people contacted after only twenty-four days as people spread the word exponentially. Indeed, after just four more days, twenty-eight days total, the number of people spoken with would exceed the population of Israel, Palestine, and the U.S. combined.[4]

To complete the story, after the fourth row of the chessboard, the inventor owned 125 tons of rice, making him the largest rice holder in the empire (that's also one grain of rice for every two people in the world). The emperor had to come up with a lot of gold to purchase that much rice for the inventor. The first row on the other side of the chessboard bankrupted the emperor, and the next row exceeded the wealth of the planet. Clearly, when one person speaks to two people, and each of those two speak with two more, it takes a very short amount of time to reach everyone who can be reached.

In practice, these kind of self-propagating chains burn themselves out either because people lose motivation or because all potential people are reached. However, Two Stars for Peace need reach only the population of Israel, Palestine, and the U.S., plus opinion leaders in Arab countries and Europe. Given one week for each exponential jump instead of one day, in just twenty-eight weeks, about half a year, everyone would have heard first-hand (as well as through the media) about the importance of Two Stars for Peace. Many new ideas spread even faster than this.

This is the job for the grassroots movement: go door-to-door, office-to-office, and table-to-table getting people excited enough about the Two Stars Plan to be willing to spread the excitement to others. The mission for the grass roots movement is to persuade one person to persuade two others, and so on. Even falling far short of universal coverage, this kind of grassroots effort will end up moving politicians in the right direction.

It is helpful to start umbrella organizations so that people have a sense of belonging. These organizations can also help the self-propagation stay on track, distribute key information, and serve as a forum for grassroots decision-making. Umbrella organizations might be named Two Stars Israel, Two Stars Palestine, and Two Stars America. Within these groups, locally-oriented individuals can coordinate their efforts through local grassroots affiliates such as Two Stars of

---

3. 2+4+8+16+32+64+128+256=512 kilos of rice
4. 15+30+60+120+240=465 Million grains or people

Upper Galilee, Two Stars of Ramallah, and Two Stars of Nebraska. Telephone trees, Internet groups, and regional conventions can all add organizational fervor and once-in-a-lifetime excitement to this historic effort.

Once the Two Stars grassroots groups are activated, they can be depended upon to get out the vote, to contact their elected representatives, and to express their opinion in a hundred different ways. All trees grow from roots. So also must the tree of peace, which arises from the grassroots of the people's will and blossoms with the merged statehood of America, Israel, and Palestine.

National Discussions

Once Two Stars grassroots organizations are formed, the subject will start to percolate in national debates. For example, members of Two Stars groups will call into radio talk shows, demonstrate in public, and write newspaper articles. Television news programs will feature explanations and assessments of the Two Stars Plan. Candidates running for office will be quizzed as to their positions on the Two Stars Plan. Imams, priests, and rabbis will lead Sabbath-day discussions of the religious implications of the fresh idea.

All the while, the grassroots groups will continue person-to-person idea-sharing until millions of people in America, Europe, and the Middle East are aware of Two Stars for Peace. As journalists and editors are touched over and over again by grassroots supporters, it is certain that magazine stories will abound. As the national debate grows more robust, Two Stars will make the cover of *Newsweek*, *Time*, the *Economist*, *Alamuna*, *Arab Week*, *Israel Business* and other influential journals worldwide.

National discussions of Two Stars for Peace will spill into university classrooms, erudite think tanks, military planning, business brainstorming, diplomatic cables, government memoranda, and, ultimately, closed-door top-level political strategy sessions. A consensus will emerge that if the other guy wants to dance, so should we. It will soon dawn upon the consciousness of each country's leadership that if Americans, Arabs, Europeans, Israelis, and Palestinians all pull together, more or less in tandem, then a brilliantly effective solution to Middle East peace can be seeded. It will also become apparent that the Two Stars Plan is so win-win for everyone—much more so than anything that came before—that everyone *would* pull together if the U.S. just shows the requisite leadership.

The American president will hear this message from the grassroots volunteers, the mass media, his official advisors, and his trusted friends. This consensus will emerge parallel to surging growth in the number of grassroots volunteers. Sometime during year one, after rounds of private discussions with Arab, European, Israeli, and Palestinian leaders, we can expect the American president to claim the initiative. The press speculation will get too intense and the information leaks too annoying. Congressmen will ask the Administration to take a public stand. Religious leadership delegations will ask for White House support. It will become undeniable that this is the decision history books will most prominently remember. A likely moment for the U.S. president to commit himself to the Two Stars Plan would be during an annual State of the Union speech. All he needs to do is to ask Congress to officially invite Israel, Palestine, and the UN to participate in Two Stars for Peace.

Congressional Invitation

Upon a presidential request, it is certain that appropriate Congressional committees would formulate a resolution that invited Israel and Palestine to become American states. This process can commence in as quickly as two to four weeks. The resolution needs to be fairly specific in terms of its conditions for statehood. It is only reasonable to let the Israelis and Palestinians be totally confident that "if they follow the directions, they'll arrive at the right house."

There are surprisingly few conditions that Congress will require. A comprehensive checklist would include:

- Submission by both states of draft state constitutions that are consistent with the U.S. Constitution.

- Acceptance by both states of the pre-1967 borders as their American statehood borders, with pre-1967 Jordanian-occupied territory, no-man zones and Gaza going to Palestine, and pre-1967 Syrian-occupied territory going to Israel.

- Acceptance by both states, on behalf of their citizens, of exclusive jurisdiction by a U.S.-funded UN Forum over pre-1950 refugee compensation claims.

There are also a few key items that Congress must include in its resolution to manifest its intent to implement the Two Stars Plan in its entirety. These provisions are:

- Assurance that all persons (i) now living in Israel or Palestine, or (ii) now stateless but born, or descended from people born, in those lands after 1918, will become U.S. citizens upon the entry of Israel and Palestine into the United States;

- Assurance that up to 70,000 new "Right of Return" visas per year will be granted to any person that provides a compelling reason (such as cultural affinity) for wanting to move to either Israel or Palestine, and that such visas will mature into U.S. citizenship upon demonstration that the individual has taken up lawful residence in Israel or Palestine and otherwise is not a person who should be excluded from citizenship; and

- Assurance that the U.S. will provide $1 billion of funding to a UN Palestinian Economic Claims Adjustment Forum (PECAF), provided that it adopts rules to ensure such money is allocated in a manner to cover all legitimate claims and that Israel and Palestine accept the exclusive, binding jurisdiction of this Forum for pre-1950 claims.

There may be a few more items that Congressional committees will want to include in the resolution, such as re-emphasizing the obvious right of free travel across Israeli-Palestinian space (including Jerusalem) or the need by all parties to respect land ownership properly registered as of a date certain (e.g., December 31, 1999). However, virtually any addition is really subsumed within the items listed above. Unresolved questions can be resolved based on the legal precedent from previous states admitted to the U.S.

One important consideration for Congress is the issue of a deadline. Invitations normally entail a date by which to reply. It is not in anyone's interests to keep the invitation open indefinitely, because that just keeps the Middle-East crisis boiling. Palestinian lives have been on hold too long, and Israelis are tired of being a hostile force. Good form also entails an appropriate amount of time to reply to an invitation. While there is much for Israelis and Palestinians to do—and to ponder—more than enough time rarely produces better results than just enough time. An overcooked fish cannot compete with a lightly done fillet. Given what humans accomplish in a year, and the natural length of that period, favorable consideration should be given to a one-year deadline for all parties to respond. In a land where wars last for days, people can certainly make peace in a year. Now that there is a systematic and equitable solution, those who want a just peace will have it.

Israeli and Palestinian State Constitution Drafting

A Congressional offer of statehood will send Two Stars grassroots movements in Israel and Palestine into overdrive. Yet some of the hardest work will require legal experts working in the quiet of a great library. Merging different legal traditions will not be easy. There are several factors encouraging the timely completion of the constitution drafting effort:

- Israelis and Palestinians have already done a lot of work on drafting national constitutions;

- All modern constitutions have a lot in common because of the universality of human rights principles such as due process (fairness) and equality under law (non-discrimination);

- There are fifty models to consider based on the constitutions of America's current fifty states;

- There are excellent Israeli and Palestinian legal scholars, as well as American law school professors who would be honored to assist; and

- The International Bar Association and the American Bar Association will certainly be generous with advice and guidance.

All the help in the world will not make it easy to finesse a Jewish state controlled by secularly-elected officials into being an officially secular state likely to be controlled by elected Jews. Nor will it be much easier to morph a liberation-movement state like Palestine into one that remains overwhelmingly progressive in policy, but carefully reserves Islamic matters to non-state religious organizations while maintaining even-handed secularity in matters of state. Yet there is reason for confidence: this is precisely where America was 200 years ago.

America began her constitutional life as a safe haven for vigorously Christian souls persecuted in Europe for their non-traditional religious beliefs. Not surprisingly, Christianity infused early American life. To this day, America is a God-fearing nation, with scant tolerance for the public atheist. Over the years she has done a good job of detailing the constitutional separation of "church and state" into a reasonable and predictable set of guidelines. Under these rules, Christians, Jews, and Moslems have all thrived in America. So, if religion can thrive at arms-length from the state in what was first envisioned as a set of avowedly Christian colonies, it can do so in Israel and Palestine as well. Israeli and Palestinian constitutional scholars could not do much better than simply replicating America's first amendment guarantees of religious freedom in their new state constitutions.

Specifics often make the abstract clearer. Must the state constitutions specifically separate church and state? No, because the U.S. federal constitution already does that and it has been interpreted to apply to all states. Can the new state constitutions provide a special role for Judaism or Islam? No, because that would be using secular state power to promote a particular religion. Truly, the messages of God are great enough not to require the bureaucratic assistance of human government. May the state constitutions declare either Friday or Saturday as a statewide holiday? Yes, because that is a matter of civic convenience in overwhelmingly Moslem and Jewish societies, respectively. May the state constitutions permit children to go to school at the school of their choice? Yes, of course. May those schools be paid for with government tax dollars? Yes, so long as it is done in a non-preferential manner.

There will be much opportunity for discussion between Israeli and Palestinian constitution drafters and interested U.S. Congressional committees. Indeed, one can expect a veritable air bridge of traffic between Washington and Jerusalem. These one-on-one discussions will enable all constitutional details to be worked out to everyone's mutual satisfaction in a timely manner.

Popular Acceptance, Fine-Tuning, and Approval

On schedule, the U.S. Congress should receive transmittals from Israel, Palestine, and the UN one year after Congress issues its invitation. The Israeli and Palestinian transmittals would include their proposed state constitutions and evidence of popular approval, such as legislative votes, popular caucus votes, and nationwide referenda. The reasonableness of one year for this process is emphasized by the fact that took less than four months to write and sign the U.S. Constitution, in a slow-moving time (summer of 1787) with few precedents (or conveniences). It should not take longer for the Israeli and Palestinian constitutions. Even Israeli elections are not active for more than two months, so this too should be adequate time for a referendum. In between the constitution drafting effort and the referendum there would be intense national legislative debate. Ideally, this process should culminate within a few months in a vote of the Knesset and Palestinian Assembly in favor of merging with the U.S. under a proposed state constitution. Such a vote could also call for a national referendum to assure popular support for the decision. Allowing two to four months for constitution drafting, two to four months for legislative action, and two to four months for a popular referendum permits Israel and Palestine each to take a positive decision within the one-year invitation period.[5]

---

5. In the horse-and-buggy days, it took just six months for Texans to vote to accept an invitation from the U.S. Congress to trade in their independent republic for the status of a U.S. state. The entire process, from firm Congressional invitation to Congressional grant of statehood based on Texas' fulfillment of conditions, took less than one year (March 1, 1845, to December 29, 1845).

It is important to bear in mind that during this entire year the Two Stars grass-roots movement would be very active. This movement will work every aspect in parallel while the Israeli and Palestinian governments proceed more serially. Grassroots groups will spawn draft constitutions for experts to consider. They will work every political party and faction to garner support in advance of upcoming legislative debates. Legions of volunteers will prepare for the referendum by spreading the word as described above. This will be a continuation of their efforts that began internationally a year earlier and led to the Congressional invitation.

Diplomats will also have to be active during the year of invitation. It can take from days to years to get a resolution out of the UN. This will be no ordinary resolution, because it will conditionally supersede over fifty years of resolutions bearing on peace in the Israeli-Palestinian space. It will also be unusual in setting up a PECAF to operate like the World Trade Center Victims Fund, but for pre-1950 Palestinian claims. Nevertheless, if there was ever a cause worthy of UN top-priority attention, this is it. There is no doubt that a comprehensive resolution can be adopted in under a year with diplomatic support from Arab and European countries, in addition to American leadership. If the Israeli and Palestinian UN representatives clearly state that this is what they want, then the Arab, European, and American representatives should feel duty-bound to play their roles.

It may well be that as the draft state constitutions arrive, or as the UN resolution arrives, new issues will have surfaced that were not satisfactorily settled in the original Congressional invitation. It will not be the first dinner invitation to which guests replied with a meal preference, or that others accepted with an extra guest or a heads-up regarding non-conforming clothing. In such case, what should Congress do? How will the Two Stars Plan handle these last-minute contingencies?

Congress should be flexible, within the basic parameters of the Two Stars Plan, about inserting additional language in its final statehood legislation that accommodates special circumstances. For example, there may be good reason to adjust the number of "Right of Return" visas.[6] It may be necessary to permit some minor variation from the pre-1967 borders, although this should be treated with

---

6. This may well be a theoretical issue, because while Israelis and Palestinians want to know they can welcome their co-ethnics home, in fact, immigration to the land has been modest. Of course, that could change with U.S. citizenship. As a benchmark, when Texas joined the U.S. in 1845 it increased the American population by about 1%, which would be about 3 million people today. Annexed states in the years shortly after Texas joined, such as California (1850) and New Mexico, made a contribution roughly equal to that of Texas.

great caution, as it could lead to endless bickering over borders—something that is no longer relevant once both states are part of the same union.

It may also be worthwhile to offer something that greases the tracks along which the merger is launched. For example, at the time California joined the United States, Congress agreed to assume the claims of residents against the previous sovereign power, Mexico, and to grant citizenship to any Mexicans residing in California.[7] In a somewhat similar vein, Congress could stipulate in its final statehood legislation, if necessary, that the U.S. would assume liability for post-1950 claims against Israel or Palestine by America's new citizens.

In Two Years It Can Be Done

Two years is enough time to implement Two Stars. Taking the formation of the first grassroots Two Stars group as day one, there should be almost universal awareness of the Two Stars Plan in six months. Many people will hear about it from a neighbor or a friend. Almost everyone will hear about it from the mass media.

After six months or so there will be a critical mass of support to place Two Stars for Peace on religious, business, government, and international agendas. From this point, another six months of discussion will enable a positive consensus to congeal in Israel, Palestine, and the United States, as well as in the Islamic world, or *umma*, and the EU. The consensus will be that the Two Stars Plan is a realistic, a just, and a better way to go. From there it is simply a matter of finding the right moment and venue for the U.S. president to claim the initiative and ask Congress to issue a formal invitation. Thus far, about a year has passed.

Congress will not need more than a month or so to draft and adopt its resolution. As noted above, Israelis, Palestinians, and the UN can all fulfill their roles within a year. For Israel and Palestine, the year will be spent developing a state constitution, debating within government and major power sectors the myriad details of implementation, and conducting a national referendum. Within two years a just peace, with dignity and promise for all concerned, can be established in the Middle East. How could we not stop what we are doing and make this happen now!

In this brief book, that which seemed hopeless has been made hopeful. Wrongs *can be* righted, refugees returned, security assured, and economic growth guaranteed. All it takes is American statehood for Israel and Palestine. Our collective

---

7. This was done in the 1850 Treaty of Guadalupe Hidalgo, ending the Mexican-American War. Interestingly, it was Henry David Thoreau's refusal to pay a tax that might have supported this war effort that led to a one-night imprisonment and his drafting of the famous essay *Civil Disobedience* (1849), a seminal text for future nonviolent movements led by Martin Luther King, Jr., and Mahatma Gandhi.

willpower is a necessary, if not sufficient, basis for this action to occur. From what willpower sows, reality grows.

In these ten chapters we have admitted the full nature of the Israeli-Palestinian problem, pushing no aspect of it to the side. No closet is large enough, not even the future itself, to hold Jerusalem, Bantustan-like provocations, millions of refugees, and the collective memory of uncompensated injuries. In these ten chapters, we describe the only truly robust solution, one with no unresolved issues spilling out of closets like gremlins in a Spielberg cartoon. This solution, American statehood for Israel and Palestine, resolves every dead-end, roadblock, and unsigned direction of the old roadmap to peace. It provides real justice to those wronged, real opportunity to those unemployed, and real peace to those whose lives are at risk. Is it not better to solve the chronic issue than to issue chronic solutions?

Two Stars for Peace solves the chronic issue like a well-built house solves one's homestead for life. Every other approach is like a house of cards, chronically in need of more cards and always at risk of collapse. The Two Stars solution stood tall when we tested it in Chapters 3 through 9 against the likely concerns or criticisms of every material constituency. It helps the great religions by providing peace, brotherhood, and freedom to worship in their holiest places. It allows Americans, Arabs, and Europeans to bask in the joy of Middle-East peace. It also enables their governments to battle nihilistic terrorism, undistracted by a back-court debate over Middle-East policies. It is affordable, politically survivable, and manifestly practical.

For the United Nations, the Two Stars Plan provides a unique opportunity to bring to a beneficent conclusion its decades-long trek for peace. By playing its role as an adjuster of claims arising from its very first actions in the Middle East, the UN will have the opportunity to demonstrate the important principle of accountability. Even more importantly, by accepting Two Stars for Peace as the satisfactory conclusion of its dozens of resolutions related to the subject, the UN will help to imbue new respect for international law.

Everything worthwhile begins with the people. In the twenty-first century, grassroots movements are the true voice of the people. So let every person, young and old, examine their life. What have I participated in of historic importance? How have I helped change the world into a better place? This is what and here is how. Take up the banner of Two Stars for Peace. Wave it high and carry it with you wherever you go. Make this social movement your social movement. Make this just peace your just peace. Make this cause your cause.

Know well that as you move on through your life, your work on Two Stars for Peace will forever bless your path. Billions of lives may be saved by saving the lives of Israelis and Palestinians today. Gargantuan good is done by disarming a big bomb at the crossroads of time. Unlimited joy is unleashed by connecting the descendants of antiquity with the titans of technology. One can virtually feel the heartfelt appreciation of a millennium to come for the unselfish actions of those at its outset. Be one of those courageous millennial pioneers; be committed members of Two Stars for Peace. Be one who had the insight to match history with equity, piety with propriety, and prudence with promise. Carry on with the warmth of wisdom and the serenity of spirit. Realize through actions that a brave new thought overwhelms a thousand tattered tales. What greater glory can life offer than this glory of the good?

Appendix A

Sample (Draft) Joint Resolution of U.S. Congress for Accepting Israel and Palestine into the United States

Begun and held at the city of Washington, in the District of Columbia, on Month, Day, Year

1. Resolved by the Senate and House of Representatives of the United States of America in Congress assembled, That Congress does consent that the territory properly included within, and rightfully belonging to Israel and Palestine, may be erected into two new American states, to be called the State of Israel and the State of Palestine, with republican forms of government, to be adopted by the peoples of said states, with the consent of the existing governments, in order that the same may be admitted as two new states of this Union.

2. And be it further resolved, that the foregoing consent of Congress is given upon the following conditions, and with the following guarantees, to wit:

First: said states to be formed in accordance with boundaries as they existed prior to the Six Day War of 1967, with the following provisos:

   a. Palestine be comprised of that territory known as the West Bank and the Gaza Strip, including that portion of Jerusalem under Jordanian control prior to the 1967 War as well as the international zones of East Jerusalem.

   b. Israel be comprised of that territory under Israeli control prior to the 1967 War, including the "no-man's zones" of Jerusalem, as well as lands captured from Syria in the Golan Heights.

c. All such borders are subject to adjustment by this government with regard to all questions of boundary that may arise with other governments, including in particular, the Golan Heights.

d. Neither state may erect checkpoints, gates or other impediments to the free flow of people and commerce between them.

Second: that the constitutions thereof, with the proper evidence of their adoption by the people of said Israel and Palestine, shall be transmitted to the President of the United States, to be laid before Congress for its final action, on or before the last day of the 12th month following the date of this resolution.

Third: said states, when admitted into the Union, after ceding to the United States all fortifications, barracks, navy and navy-yards, aircraft, missiles, arms, armaments, and all other property and means pertaining to the public defense, shall retain all the public funds, debts, taxes, and dues of every kind which may belong to or be due and owing said Israel and Palestine.

Fourth: said states, when admitted into the Union, shall be admitted on an equal basis with all other states and, pending the decennial census in 2010, shall be allocated two seats each in the U.S. Senate and eight seats to Israel plus four seats to Palestine in the House of Representatives, such division reflecting current population estimates of each state.

Fifth: to accommodate legislative representative of said states, with minimal disruption to current legislative representation, Congress shall adopt legislation when admitting said states to the Union that increases at that time the size of the House of Representatives by 12 seats, to 447 seats total, and further increases the size of the House of Representatives to 450 seats in 2012 to accommodate reapportionment based upon the 2010 decennial census.

Sixth: to provide assurance with regard to citizenship and rights of return, upon admitting said states to the Union the following persons shall be deemed U.S. citizens with a right of residence in the state of their choice:

a. Persons currently citizens of Israel or Palestine;

b. Persons born, or descended from persons born, in Israel or Palestine subsequent to 1920 but now currently stateless, together with their immediate family; and

c. Persons with a compelling reason to live permanently in Israel or Palestine, such as ancestral roots, who demonstrate lawful residence as such pursuant to a new "territorial reunion" visa that will be awarded in adequate number each year by U.S. embassies worldwide.

Seventh: in order to regularize and harmonize international law relating to Israel and Palestine, upon admission of said states to the Union, and upon adoption by the United Nations of a resolution that satisfies the two following conditions, $1 billion shall be transferred to the United Nations for the express purposes set forth below:

a. A UN resolution shall recognize equal statehood of Israel and Palestine within the United States as fulfillment of its previous boundary-related resolutions relating to Israel and Palestine.

b. A UN resolution shall establish a Palestinian Claims Adjustment Forum with operating rules that provide for it to equitably allocate $1 billion among all likely claimants for losses incurred as a direct result of the 1948 Partition of the British Mandate in Palestine, including changes to borders through the date of the 1949 Armistice.

Eighth: In order to facilitate the integration of Israel and Palestine into the United States, upon admission of said states to the Union, the government shall assume liability for claims of citizens of either state against either state for unlawful deprivation of life, liberty, or property subsequent to the 1949 Armistice.

3. Then, Be it resolved, upon satisfaction of the aforesaid conditions and implementation of the aforesaid guarantees, that two states, to be formed out of the present boundaries of Israel and Palestine, with suitable extent and boundaries, and with representatives in Congress as specified above, until the 2012 apportionment of representation, shall be admitted into the Union, by virtue of legislation implementing this resolution, on an equal footing with the existing states.

4. And be it further resolved that the President of the United States is invited to offer this Joint Resolution of Congress to the leaders of Israel and Palestine and to convey to such leaders that this Joint Resolutions is an invitation from the People of the United States to the Peoples of Israel and Palestine to join this Union as its 51st and 52nd states.

Appendix B

Joint Resolution for annexing Texas to the United States

28th Congress Second Session

Begun and held at the city of Washington, in the District of Columbia, on Monday the second day of December, eighteen hundred and forty-four.

1. Resolved by the Senate and House of Representatives of the United States of America in Congress assembled, That Congress doth consent that the territory properly included within, and rightfully belonging to the Republic of Texas, may be erected into a new state, to be called the state of Texas, with a republican form of government, to be adopted by the people of said republic, by deputies in Convention assembled, with the consent of the existing government, in order that the same may be admitted as one of the states of this Union.

2. And be it further resolved, That the foregoing consent of Congress is given upon the following conditions, and with the following guarantees, to wit: First—said state to be formed, subject to the adjustment by this government of all questions of boundary that may arise with other governments; and the constitution thereof, with the proper evidence of its adoption by the people of said republic of Texas, shall be transmitted to the President of the United States, to be laid before Congress for its final action, on or before the first day of January, one thousand eight hundred and forty-six. Second—said state, when admitted into the Union, after ceding to the United States all public edifices, fortifications, barracks, ports and harbors, navy and navy-yards, docks, magazines, arms, armaments, and all other property and means pertaining to the public defense belonging to said republic of Texas, shall retain all the public funds, debts, taxes, and dues of every kind which may belong to or be due and owing said republic; and shall also retain all the vacant and unappropriated lands lying within its limits, to be applied to

the payment of the debts and liabilities of said republic of Texas; and the residue of said lands, after discharging said debts and liabilities, to be disposed of as said state may direct; but in no event are said debts and liabilities to become a charge upon the government of the United States. Third—New states, of convenient size, not exceeding four in number, in addition to said state of Texas, and having sufficient population, may hereafter, by the consent of said state, be formed out of the territory thereof, which shall be entitled to admission under the provisions of the federal constitution. And such states as may be formed out of that portion of said territory lying south of thirty-six degrees thirty minutes north latitude, commonly known as the Missouri compromise line, shall be admitted into the Union with or without slavery, as the people of each state asking admission may desire. And in such state or states as shall be formed out of said territory north of said Missouri compromise line, slavery, or involuntary servitude, (except for crime,) shall be prohibited.

3. And be it further resolved, That if the President of the United States shall in his judgment and discretion deem it most advisable, instead of proceeding to submit the foregoing resolution to the Republic of Texas, as an overture on the part of the United States for admission, to negotiate with that Republic; then, Be it resolved, that a state, to be formed out of the present Republic of Texas, with suitable extent and boundaries, and with two representatives in Congress, until the next apportionment of representation, shall be admitted into the Union, by virtue of this act, on an equal footing with the existing states, as soon as the terms and conditions of such admission, and the cession of the remaining Texan territory to the United States shall be agreed upon by the governments of Texas and the United States: And that the sum of one hundred thousand dollars be, and the same is hereby, appropriated to defray the expenses of missions and negotiations, to agree upon the terms of said admission and cession, either by treaty to be submitted to the Senate, or by articles to be submitted to the two Houses of Congress, as the President may direct.

J W JONES
Speaker of the House of Representatives.

WILLIE P. MANGUM
President, pro tempore, of the Senate.

Approv'd March 1, 1845

APPENDIX C

Final Admission of Texas into the United States

Whereas the Congress of the United States, by a joint resolution approved March the first, eighteen hundred and forty-five, did consent that the territory properly included within, and rightfully belonging to, the Republic of Texas, might be erected into a new State, to be called The State of Texas, with a republican form of government, to be adopted by the people of said republic, by deputies in convention assembled, with the consent of the existing government, in order that the same might be admitted as one of the States of the Union; which consent of Congress was given upon certain conditions specified in the first and second sections of said joint resolution; and whereas the people of the said Republic of Texas, by deputies in convention assembled, with the consent of the existing government, did adopt a constitution, and erect a new State with a republican form of government, and, in the name of the people of Texas, and by their authority, did ordain and declare that they assented to and accepted the proposals, conditions, and guaranties contained in said first and second sections of said resolution: and whereas the said constitution, with the proper evidence of its adoption by the people of the Republic of Texas, has been transmitted to the President of the United States and laid before Congress, in conformity to the provisions of said joint resolution:

Therefore—
Resolved by the Senate and House of Representatives of the United States of America in Congress assembled, That the State of Texas shall be one, and is hereby declared to be one, of the United States of America, and admitted into the Union on an equal footing with the original States in all respects whatever.

Sec. 2. And be it further resolved, That until the representatives in Congress shall be apportioned according to an actual enumeration of the inhabitants of the United States, the State of Texas shall be entitled to choose two representatives.

Approved, December 29, 1845

APPENDIX D

Map Based on Rhodes Armistice of 1949, Including Detail of Jerusalem (Pre-1967 Borders of Israel and Palestinian Land, Then Occupied by Jordan and Egypt)

The Rhodes Armistice Line, 1949

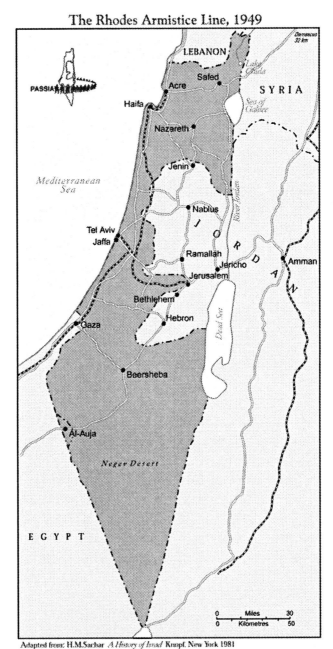

Adapted from: H.M.Sachar *A History of Israel* Knopf. New York 1981

Palestinian Academic Society for the Study of International Affairs (PASSIA)

Partitioned Jerusalem, 1948 -1967

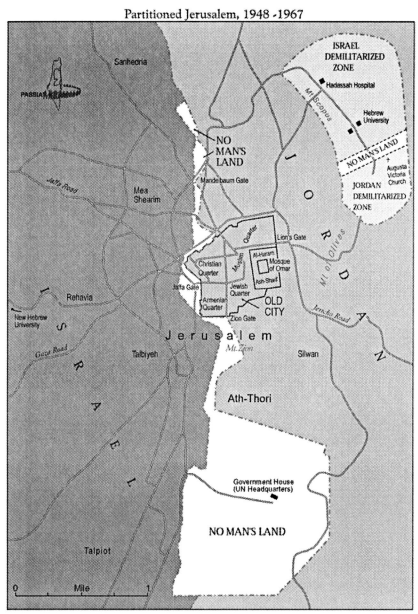

Source: H.M.Sacher *A History of Israel*, Knopf 1979

APPENDIX E

A Few Facts and Assumptions

Category	America	Israel	Palestine
Population	280MM	6MM	3MM
Diaspora	N/A	8MM	5MM
Diaspora In U.S.	N/A	5MM	350K
Net Diaspora	N/A	3MM	4.6MM
GNP	$10 Trillion	$100B	N/A
U.S. Senate	104*	2*	2*
U.S. House	447**	8*	6*
Electors	550*	10*	6*

* Proposed, and House seats to be adjusted based on decennial U.S. census in 2010.
** Proposed, and to be increased to 450 in 2012.

Martine Rothblatt
1110 Spring Street
Silver Spring, MD 20910
301-608-9292
mar@unither.com

0-595-65982-9

Printed in the United States
1435000002BC/1-33

9 780595 659821